Progress, Not Perfection

A Progressive Christian Journey Through the 12 Steps of Alcoholics Anonymous

under the supervision of
Damian Geddry

Theological Essentials

©Digital Theological Library 2025
Library of Congress Cataloging-in-Publication Data

Damian Geddry (creator).
Progress, Not Perfection: A Progressive Christian Journey Through the 12 Steps of Alcoholics Anonymous / Damian Geddry
124 + xii pp. cm. 12.7 x 20.32
ISBN 979-8-89731-977-0 (Print)
ISBN 979-8-89731-165-1 (Ebook)
ISBN 979-8-89731-152-1 (Kindle)
ISBN 979-8-89731-163-7 (Abridged Audio Discussion)

       1 Twelve-step programs — Religious aspects — Christianity 2 Christianity and alcoholics
       3 Alcoholics — Religious life

BV4596.T88 G43 2025

Second Printing

This book is available in other languages at www.DTLPress.com

Cover Image: "A Bright Future Ahead" Image produced by the author using AI

Contents

Series Preface
ix

Part I
Recovery in the Context of the 12 Steps and Progressive Christianity

Introduction
Between "Higher Power" and "God"
3

Chapter 1
The Spirit Behind the Steps
7

Chapter 2
Progressive Christianity 101
11

Chapter 3
What Is a Higher Power?
15

Part II
The Twelve Steps
A Progressive Christian Journey

Chapter 4
Step One – Admitting Powerlessness as Sacred Ground
23

Chapter 5
Step Two – Coming to Believe
27

Chapter 6
Step Three — Turning Over, Not Giving Up
33

Chapter 7
Step Four — A Searching and Fearless Moral Inventory
37

Chapter 8
Step Five — Confession as Freedom
43

Chapter 9
Step Six — Ready for Change
49

Chapter 10
Step Seven — Humbly Asked God
55

Chapter 11
Step Eight — Making the List
61

Chapter 12
Step Nine — Making Amends
65

Chapter 13
Step Ten — Daily Cleaning
71

Chapter 14
Step Eleven — Conscious Contact
75

Chapter 15
Step Twelve — The Awakening
81

Epilogue to Part II
The Steps Are a Spiral, Not a Straight Line
85

Part III
Living Grace Forward in Progressive Recovery

Chapter 16
When God Still Feels Complicated
89

Chapter 17
Beyond Belief
91

Chapter 18
Creating Communities of Healing
93

Part IV
Theological Reflections on the 12 Steps

Chapter 19
Why Theology Matters in Recovery
97

Chapter 20
Traditional and Progressive
Christianity Compared on the 12 Steps
101

Chapter 21
Process Theology
Applied to the 12 Steps
109

Chapter 22
Open and Relational Theology (ORT) and the 12 Steps
115

Conclusion
A Spacious and Loving God for the Journey
121

Series Preface

Artificial Intelligence (AI) is changing everything, including theological scholarship and education. This series, *Theological Essentials*, is designed to bring the creative potential of AI to the field of theological education. In the traditional model, a scholar with both mastery of the scholarly discourse and a record of successful classroom teaching would spend several months—or even several years—writing, revising and rewriting an introductory text which would then be transferred to a publisher who also invested months or years in production processes. Even though the end product was typically quite predictable, this slow and expensive process caused the prices of textbooks to balloon. As a result, students in developed nations paid more than they should have for the books and students in developing nations typically had no access to these (cost-prohibitive) textbooks until they appeared as discards and donations decades later. In previous generations, the need for quality assurance—in the form of content generation, expert review, copy-editing and printing time—may have made this slow, expensive and exclusionary approach inevitable. However, AI is changing everything.

This series is very different; it is created by AI. The cover of each volume identifies the work as "created under the supervision of" an expert in the field. However, that person is not an author in the traditional sense. The creator of each volume has been trained by the DTL staff in the use of AI and *the creator has used AI to create, edit, revise and recreate the text that you see*. With that creation process clearly identified, let me explain the goals of this series.

Our Goals:
Credibility: Although AI has made—and continues to make—huge strides over the last few years, no unsupervised AI can create a truly reliable or fully credible college or seminary level text. The limitations of AI generated content sometimes originates from the limitations of the content itself (the training set may be inadequate), but more often, user dissatisfaction with AI-generated content arises from human errors associated with poor prompt engineering. The DTL Press has sought to overcome both of these problems by hiring established scholars with widely recognized expertise to create books within their areas of expertise and by training those scholars and experts in AI prompt engineering. To be clear, the scholar whose name appears on the cover of this work has created this volume—generating, reading, regenerating, rereading and revising the work. Even though the work was generated (in varying degrees) by AI, the names of our scholarly creators appear on the cover as a guarantee that the content is equally credible with any introductory work which that scholar/creator would pen using the traditional model.

Stability: AI is generative, meaning that the response to each prompt is uniquely generated for that specific request. No two AI-generated responses are precisely the same. The inevitable variability of AI responses presents a significant pedagogical challenge for professors and students who wish to begin their discussions and analysis on the basis of a shared set of ideas. Educational institutions need stable texts in order to prevent pedagogical chaos. These books provide that stable text from which to teach, discuss and engage ideas.

Affordability: The DTL Press is committed to the idea that affordability should not be a barrier to knowledge. *All persons are equally deserving of the right to know and to understand.* Therefore, ebook versions of all DTL Press books are available from the DTL libraries without charge, and available as print books for a nominal fee. Our scholar/creators are to be thanked for their willingness to forego traditional royalty arrangements. (Our creators are compensated for their generative work, but they do not receive royalties in the traditional sense.)

Accessibility: The DTL Press would like to make high quality, low cost introductory textbooks available to everyone, everywhere in the world. The books in this series are immediately made available in multiple languages. The DTL Press will create translations in other languages upon request. Translations are, of course, generated by AI.

Our Acknowledged Limitations:

Some readers are undoubtedly thinking, "but AI can only produce derivative scholarship; AI can't create original, innovative scholarship." That criticism is, of course, largely accurate. AI is largely limited to aggregating, organizing and repackaging pre-existing ideas (although sometimes in ways that can be used to accelerate and refine the production of original scholarship). Still while acknowledging this inherent limitation of AI, the DTL Press would offer two comments: (1) Introductory texts are seldom meant to be truly ground breaking in their originality and (2) the DTL Press has other series dedicated to publishing original scholarship with traditional authorship.

Our Invitation:

The DTL Press would like to fundamentally reshape academic publishing in the theological world to make scholarship more accessible and more affordable in two ways. First, we would like to generate introductory texts in all areas of theological discourse, so that no one is ever forced to "buy a textbook" in any language. It is our vision for professors anywhere to be able to use one book, two books or an entire set of books in this series as the *introductory* textbooks for their classes. Second, we would also like to publish traditionally authored scholarly monographs for Open Access (free) distribution for an advanced scholarly readership.

Finally, the DTL Press is non-confessional and will publish works in any area of religious studies. Traditionally authored books are peer-reviewed; AI-generated introductory book creation is open to anyone with the required expertise to supervise content generation in that area of discourse. If you share the DTL Press's commitment to credibility, affordability and accessibility, contact us about changing the world of theological publishing by contributing to this series or a more traditionally authored series.

With high expectations,
Thomas E. Phillips
DTL Press Executive Director
www.thedtl.org

Part I
Recovery in the Context of the 12 Steps and Progressive Christianity

Introduction
Between "Higher Power" and "God"

"Made a decision to turn our will and our lives over to the care of God <u>as we understood Him</u>."
— *Step 3 of Alcoholics Anonymous*

There's a moment in almost every 12-step meeting when the word "God" is spoken. And in that moment, something stirs in the room. For some, it's comfort — a word they've clung to in desperation. For others, it's a red flag — a reminder of religious wounds, exclusion, or spiritual baggage. And for many, it's simply confusing: Who or what is this God we're talking about?

If you've ever felt caught between the vagueness of "a higher power" and the rigidity of a traditional religion that posits God as "Him," this short, introductory book is for you.

A Spirituality That's Honest, Not Evasive

The 12 Steps of Alcoholics Anonymous invite people into spiritual transformation. But that journey can feel disjointed when the language is either too empty or too confining. "Higher Power" may feel like a placeholder for anything — a doorknob, the ocean, the AA group itself. But "God" as a bearded judge in the clouds, or as a narrow religious or theological box, can be equally alienating.

Progressive Christianity offers another way. It doesn't throw out God. It doesn't flatten all spiritual paths into vague sameness. Instead, it dares to believe that Jesus shows us what a truly loving, liberating, and grace-filled God looks like — and that this God is not afraid of our doubts, wounds, or messy recoveries.

We Are All in Recovery

This book isn't just about addiction. It's about transformation. It's about the way we all — addicted or not — need to surrender our illusions, take moral inventory, make amends, and seek something greater than our own egos.

The 12 Steps are a map. Scripture is a companion. And Jesus? He's not a taskmaster. He's a guide who walks every step with us, even when we're limping, resisting, backsliding or unsure.

What You'll Find in This Book

First, there are several short chapters explaining the spiritual orientation of the book, and how that orientation and language applies to each of AA's 12 Steps.

Each following chapter then explores one of the 12 Steps through a progressive Christian lens. In this brief unpacking of each step, you'll find:

- *Honest reflections on what the step means — spiritually, emotionally, and practically*
- *Biblical references and verses that illuminate the step (but never weaponize them)*
- *Personal questions for self-reflection or group discussion*
- *Short prayers or meditations to help you reflect on what you've just read*

At the end, an addendum gives a brief, introductory overview of three theological models: progressive Christianity compared to more traditional Christianity as they relate to each of the 12 Steps, and then separate sections that apply Process Theology and then Open-and-Relational Theology to the 12 Steps. These sections are meant to give you three unique lenses with which to approach the Steps.

Regardless, you don't need to be a theologian to move through this book. You don't need to be sure what you believe. You just need to be open hearted and open minded — willing.

Whether you're in recovery, supporting someone who is, or simply curious about how faith and healing intersect, this book is an invitation. Not to certainty — but to connection. Not to dogma — but to grace.

Chapter 1
The Spirit Behind the Steps

"God, grant me the serenity…"
— *The Serenity Prayer*

When Bill Wilson and the early founders of Alcoholics Anonymous developed the 12 Steps in the 1930s, they weren't trying to start a spiritual revolution. They were simply desperate men seeking a way to stay sober — and they stumbled upon something that worked: surrender, community, self-honesty, and a power beyond themselves.

But that "power" was never precisely defined. And that was intentional. And remarkable.

A Spiritual Program Without a Specific Theology

The 12 Steps reference "God" four times, and speak more often of a "Power greater than ourselves." But *The Big Book* of AA also insists: "We have no monopoly on God." The program was never meant to be religious, though it's deeply spiritual.

This flexibility has helped millions. It's why an atheist, a Buddhist, and a Christian can all sit in the same circle and hear something true. But it's also why some people get stuck — because "God as you understand Him" can feel too vague to be meaningful… while the God they grew up with may be too harsh to be healing.

So where does that leave us?

The Problem with "God"

Some of us come into recovery with a sense of God — but it's a God who's disappointed in us, who's been silent during our worst moments, or who has been used to shame and control us. For others, God was never part of the equation. Maybe religion was oppressive. Maybe it just never felt real.

Yet the 12 Steps seem to assume we'll find something... someone... beyond ourselves. A higher power. A source of wisdom. A well of strength we can't produce alone.

So how do we move forward spiritually when "God" is a word that hurts — or feels hollow?

A Progressive Christian Lens

Progressive Christianity begins not with certainty, but with love, compassion and understanding.

It honors the authority and example of Jesus — not because he fits a theological box, but because he breaks them open. It reads Scripture seriously, but not literally. It believes in grace, not because we're sinful wretches, but because we're sacred beings who forget who we are.

Most importantly, it sees recovery not as a detour from faith, but as a sacred path itself.

What if we stopped trying to reconcile the God of AA with the God of many churches, and instead looked at Jesus — the one who healed the sick, ate with addicts, welcomed the outcast, and told religious people to chill out?

What if he is the face of the Higher Power we're meant to encounter in the steps?

The Spirit Beneath the Steps

Here's the deeper truth: the 12 Steps are not about getting religion. They're about getting real.

- *Step 1 is about telling the truth.*
- *Step 2 is about hope.*

- *Step 3 is about letting go of control.*
- *Step 4 is about self-examination with compassion.*
- *Step 5 is about confession and connection.*
- *And so on.*

These are spiritual acts — whether we name them "Christian" or not.

But for those of us who do seek Jesus in the process, we may find he's already been there. Not waiting at the finish line, but walking with us step by step. Not demanding perfection, but offering presence.

Grace Along the Path

Grace is the heartbeat of recovery — not just a theological idea, but an everyday reality. In progressive Christian terms, grace is the unearned, unconditional love of God — the kind that meets us not after we change, but as we are. In fact, it meets us so that we can change. In recovery, grace often comes disguised:

- *As the voice on the other end of a late-night call who says, "You're not alone."*
- *As the unexpected strength to get through a hard day without drinking or using.*
- *As a moment of laughter in a room full of pain.*
- *As the simple gift of waking up sober and breathing without shame.*

Grace doesn't always feel loud or emotional. Sometimes it's quiet, steady, and ordinary — the sense that something is holding you when you want to fall apart. Sometimes grace sounds like someone else telling their story, and you suddenly realizing, "Me too." Sometimes it looks like mercy in the mirror.

Grace says you don't have to earn your healing. You just have to receive it. And when you do, even in pieces, it becomes the power that carries you from Step One all the way forward.

In the 12-Step path, grace is never far away. It lives in surrender, in community, in truth-telling, in forgiveness. And most of all, it lives in the steady return — step by step — to a God who never stopped walking with you.

Recovery Is a Spiritual Awakening

If God has been a problem for you — you're in good company. The Gospels are full of people trying to make sense of who God is, what God wants, and whether they're included. Jesus never asked for perfect theology. He asked for openness. He offered healing. He sat down at tables others wouldn't.

And that's what progressive Christianity and this book aim to do: sit at that table with you.

We'll walk through each step, reflect on its meaning, explore the wisdom of Scripture, and ask where God — the loving, liberating, human God revealed in Christ — might be showing up.

You don't need to believe everything. You don't need to call it "God" if you're not ready. Just be willing to keep showing up. Take what you want and leave the rest.

Chapter 2
Progressive Christianity 101

"You shall know the truth, and the truth shall set you free."
— John 8:32

For many people in recovery, faith is either a lifeline or a landmine. You may come to the 12 Steps feeling spiritually hungry — or spiritually hurt. Maybe you've walked away from church. Maybe you've never been part of one. Maybe you've had God used against you, or you were told your questions and even your curiosity made you a heretic.

But what if faith doesn't have to look like that? What if Christianity — at its core — isn't about rules, fear, or narrow theology, but about healing, truth-telling, and radical grace?

That's the heart of progressive Christianity.

What Makes Christianity "Progressive"?

Progressive Christianity isn't a new religion. It's an old story told in a spacious way. It's Christianity that affirms:

- *Jesus is the center, but not a weapon.*
- *The Bible is sacred, but not a rulebook.*
- *Faith is a journey, not a test you pass or fail.*
- *God is love, and love doesn't exclude, shame, or abandon.*
- *Spirituality and justice are inseparable — we don't just pray, we care for the poor, the hurting, and the outcast.*

- *Doubt is not the enemy of faith — it's often the beginning of it.*

In short, progressive Christianity trusts that God is still speaking, and that God is more concerned with how we live than what boxes we check.

This is not Christianity that demands you believe six impossible things before breakfast. It's Christianity that walks with you, listens, and points gently toward a Christ who heals, liberates, and loves unconditionally — including the parts of you still in process. Hence the important phrase "progress rather than perfection."

Jesus and the Wounded

In the Gospels, Jesus rarely lectures. He touches, forgives, feeds, weeps, and welcomes. He is constantly breaking religious rules to make room for people in need of hope and healing.

- *He touches lepers when no one else will.*
- *He eats with drunkards and sinners.*
- *He defends women society condemned.*
- *He tells stories where the hero is the outsider.*
- *Jesus doesn't demand purity before presence.*
- *He brings presence that leads to healing.*

If you're in recovery and unsure about God, that's okay. If you're unsure about church, you're in good company — Jesus often was too. What matters is that you're open to the possibility that *love is bigger than your shame*, that *healing is more powerful than guilt, and that God is already working in your life*, even if you don't have a name for it yet.

Faith in a God Who Feels

Progressive Christianity draws on a vision of God that is not removed or indifferent — but deeply relational. In theological terms, this often echoes process theology or open and relational theology, which says God is not a puppeteer in the sky, but a Presence that suffers with us, evolves with us, and invites us into growth moment by moment. In the recovery context, this means:

- *God isn't waiting to punish you for your past.*
- *God isn't micromanaging your cravings or your slips.*
- *God is a persuasive rather than a coercive influence in your recovery.*
- *God is in the process — in the meetings, the honesty, the surrender, and the slow rebuild of your life.*

It's not about fixing your beliefs. It's about learning to trust again — yourself, others, and the deeper current of grace holding you through it all. It's about the subtle lure of a higher power.

Scripture as Story, Not Weapon

You may have had Scripture quoted at you like a club or rigid set of requirements and rules. That's not how we'll use it here.

In this book, the Bible is a conversation partner, not an answer key. It's full of stories of broken people who find healing, of failure turned to faith, of exile turned into homecoming. It doesn't offer easy answers, but it does offer deep truth — the kind you discover as you live it out. Like life, the Bible is a series of challenges and revelations.

We'll draw from these stories in every step. Not to prove anything, but to help you see yourself in a much bigger, more optimistic and evolving story.

A Faith That Walks with You

Progressive Christianity doesn't ask you to abandon AA's openness. It honors it — and adds a voice to the mix. A voice that says:

- *God is not afraid of your addiction.*
- *God is not disappointed in your questions.*
- *God is not angry with your past.*
- *God is not limited by rigid theology.*
- *God is with you — right here, right now — exactly as you are.*

So, as we begin walking through the 12 Steps together, remember: this isn't a test of belief. It's an invitation to healing. You don't need to be "spiritually advanced." You just need to be open.

Chapter 3
What Is a Higher Power?

"Came to believe that a Power greater than ourselves could restore us to sanity."
— Step 2 of Alcoholics Anonymous

It's one of the strangest sentences in early recovery: *"You don't have to believe in God — just a Higher Power."* For some, this is a gift: "Finally, I can breathe. I don't have to buy into a religion." For others, it's frustrating: "What does that even mean? An app on my phone? A therapist? The ocean? A group of strangers in a church basement?"

And for some of us who grew up Christian — especially in rigid, guilt-heavy versions — it raises a bigger question: Can I trust any 'higher power' at all? This short chapter can be helpful if:

- *You're skeptical of vague spirituality.*
- *You've been burned by organized religion.*
- *You're open, but confused by all the God-talk.*
- *You want something more than metaphor… but more loving than the God you were taught to fear.*

Let's explore what a Higher Power might actually look like — and how Jesus, reimagined through a progressive lens, can meet us in this moment of searching.

Power Greater Than Ourselves

The Big Book of AA was written by people who hit bottom. Not just "drank too much" — but shattered their lives. And they discovered something radical:

They couldn't fix themselves or their situation with willpower alone.

Something outside them — greater than them — had to do the heavy lifting. That "Power greater than ourselves" didn't have to be a church-approved God. It just had to be real enough to lean on. It had to restore sanity, connection, hope, and humility. That was the test.

So, AA left the definition open — and that openness is both its strength and its surprisingly productive and revealing struggle. Something truly worth the fight because it's your discovery.

So… What Is a Higher Power? Let's break it down. A Higher Power is:

- *Something greater than your ego.*
- *Something more reliable than your cravings.*
- *Something that loves truth more than image and posturing.*
- *Something that draws you toward healing, connection, and honesty.*

In AA, people have called their Higher Power:

- *The recovery group itself*
- *Nature or the ocean*
- *Love*
- *The Universe*
- *The rhythm of life*
- *A sense of inner wisdom*
- *A nontraditional image of God (feminine, nonbinary, Christ-like, etc.)*
- *And yes, sometimes — a literal God, deeply personal and kind*

The point isn't what you call it. The point is: Does it help you get honest, stay clean and sober, and live with integrity?

Jesus as a Higher Power (Without the Baggage)

So what about those of us drawn to Jesus — but not to the hierarchal God we were raised with?

Progressive Christianity says you can trust Jesus as a window into God, without needing to accept every theological claim ever made in his name.

What if Jesus isn't your judge but your companion? What if Christ is not a gatekeeper but a guide? What if the power greater than yourself is a person who weeps when you weep, heals what you've buried, and keeps inviting you to a better, more fulfilling future?

That's a kind of power that restores sanity — not through control, but through compassion. You don't need to have your Christology, your understanding of Christ in Jesus, figured out. You just need a spiritual center big enough to steady you — and human enough to meet you in the darkness, shame and uncertainty.

Can the Group Be a Higher Power?

Yes. The AA group (or any recovery fellowship) can be a Higher Power — and for many, it's the first one that works. Why? Because:

- *It tells the truth.*
- *It loves you without needing you to perform.*
- *It holds your story without fixing it.*
- *It models transformation.*
- *It has collective wisdom and experience.*

The group is not God, but it becomes a living expression of grace. For some, this is what's meant by body of Christ. For others, it is the epitome of the early church, and a very real model for today.

"Where two or three are gathered…" (Matthew 18:20) — not a promise of doctrine, but of compassionate presence. Collective care.

What If You're Still Not Sure?

Then you're in the perfect place to practice Step 2. You don't need full belief. You need *willingness, openness and curiosity*. That's the secret. You don't have to figure it all out. Just ask:

- *What do I hope is true about the universe?*
- *What kind of love or loving power would I want to believe in?*
- *What might it feel like to trust something bigger than my own willpower?*
- *What would it feel like to be spiritually surprised?*

This isn't about magical thinking. It's about spiritual honesty. You're not looking for someone to wave a wand. You're looking for a deeper connection that can anchor you and help you move forward when everything else falls apart.

A Prayer for the Uncertain

God, Higher Power, Love, Mystery —
I'm willing to believe you might be real.
I'm tired of running the show.
Show me something steadier than myself.
Something kinder.
Something stronger.
Something that calls me back to life.
If you're out there —
— Or right here.
I'm listening.
Listening.

Time to Begin

Now we are ready to start working our way through the 12 Steps; one-by-one, chapter-by-chapter, with an understanding of God, Spirit or Higher Power as experienced and expressed through a progressive

Christian lens. A power that knows where you are and accepts you without judgment.

Part II
The Twelve Steps
A Progressive Christian Journey

Chapter 4
Step One — Admitting Powerlessness as Sacred Ground

"We admitted we were powerless over alcohol — that our lives had become unmanageable."
— Step One of Alcoholics Anonymous

There is no spiritual growth without truth. And the truth is: we tried to control everything. Our drinking. Our drug use. Our image. Our pain. Our people. Our past. It didn't work.

Step One is where the performance ends and the healing begins.

The Myth of Control

Many of us spent years trying to manage our lives through sheer effort. We masked the chaos. We downplayed the consequences. We convinced ourselves we had it handled — or would soon enough.

But addiction, whether to alcohol, drugs, work, control, perfectionism, anger, sex or shame itself, doesn't care about our best intentions.

Eventually, the wheels come off and we crash. And when we do, we face the terrifying truth:

- *We are not in control.*
- *Not of our impulses.*
- *Not of our outcomes.*
- *Not even of our image anymore.*

It feels like failure. But in reality, it's the first holy step toward freedom.

What Christianity Gets Right (and Wrong) About Powerlessness

Traditional Christianity often talks about sin and surrender, but too often, that kind of talk gets weaponized. People are told they're "nothing without God," or that powerlessness is a form of profound moral weakness. That's not what Step One is about.

In the Gospels, Jesus doesn't shame people for being powerless — he honors them for being honest.

- *The bleeding woman touches his robe in desperation — and he calls her "daughter."*
- *The thief on the cross admits his guilt — and Jesus promises him paradise.*
- *Peter breaks down after denying Jesus — and is restored with gentleness, not guilt.*

Over and over, Jesus responds to powerlessness not with condemnation, but compassion. When we stop pretending, he starts healing.

Powerlessness as Sacred Ground

Step One isn't weakness. It's clarity. It says: I cannot do this on my own anymore. My way isn't working. My attempts to control have failed. I need help. I need grace. I need something greater than me. And this honesty — raw, trembling, sometimes terrifying — becomes sacred ground.

In Exodus 3, when Moses meets God at the burning bush, he's told to remove his sandals because he's standing on holy ground. He's overwhelmed, unsure, reluctant. But that's where his call begins.

Your holy ground may not have flames, but it's just as real:

- *The floor of a detox center.*
- *The seat in a 12-step meeting.*

- *The moment you look in the mirror and say, "I can't keep doing this."*
- *That's where God meets you.*
- *Not when you're fixed — but when you're finally honest.*

Progressive Christian Theology of Surrender

Here's the paradox of grace: *You don't have to be strong to be saved.* Progressive Christianity teaches that God is not a distant authority demanding submission — but a loving Presence who walks with us in our undoing.

In 2 Corinthians 12, Paul writes that God's power is made perfect in weakness. That's not poetic exaggeration. It's experiential truth. Recovery doesn't begin when you finally "get it together." It begins when you let yourself fall apart — in the presence of something safe enough to hold you.

That's what a Higher Power offers. That's what God, as revealed in Jesus, embodies.

What This Step Is Not

Let's be clear about what Step One doesn't mean:

- *It doesn't mean you're worthless.*
- *It doesn't mean you're doomed.*
- *It doesn't mean you'll always be broken.*
- *It doesn't mean you should be passive or give up on change.*

It means you're telling the truth about your limits. And from that truth, something sacred can grow.

Scripture for Step One

"Come to me, all you who are weary and carrying heavy burdens, and I will give you rest." (Matthew 11:28)

"For when I am weak, then I am strong." (2 Corinthians 12:10)

"Create in me a clean heart, O God, and renew a right spirit within me." (Psalm 51:10)

"And when Jesus looked at the crowds, he felt sorry for them, because they were harassed and dejected, like sheep without a shepherd." (Matthew 9:36)

Reflection Questions

What have I tried to control that is now clearly unmanageable?

What would it mean to admit powerlessness without shame?

How does it feel to imagine God meeting me in my weakness, not after I overcome it?

What am I afraid will happen if I let go of control?

A Step One Prayer

God, I admit it. I can't do this alone.
I've tried. I've failed.
And I'm tired of pretending I'm fine.
Help me let go of the illusion of control.
Help me trust that I don't need to fix this before I come to you.
This is me, as I am.
And I'm ready to begin.
Help me.
Please.

Chapter 5
Step Two — Coming to Believe
The Hope Hidden in the Wreckage

"Came to believe that a Power greater than ourselves could restore us to sanity."
— Step 2 of Alcoholics Anonymous

Step One is the crash. Step Two is the possibility that something — or Someone — might still meet us in the rubble.

If Step One is about admitting powerlessness, Step Two is about not giving up. It's the spiritual "maybe."

- *Maybe I'm not beyond healing.*
- *Maybe love is real.*
- *Maybe there's a kind of power that doesn't crush, but restores.*
- *Maybe God is different than I thought.*
- *Maybe I need to get out of the way.*

This step doesn't ask for certainty. It asks for willingness — and that willingness is the seed of hope.

What Does "Sanity" Even Mean?

Many people hear "restore us to sanity" and flinch. Am I insane? Is that what AA thinks? But in the context of addiction — or any destructive cycle — "insanity" isn't about diagnosis. It's about repetition:

- *Repeating behaviors that hurt us.*
- *Denying obvious consequences.*
- *Thinking we can control something that clearly controls us.*

- *Forgetting what happened the last time.*

In recovery, sanity means clarity, peace, presence, and connection. It's living in reality instead of hiding from it. It's moving from chaos to calm — not all at once, but moment by moment.

And it starts with believing that change is possible.

Faith Without the Fine Print

Step Two doesn't say, "Came to believe in the God of your childhood." It doesn't say, "Came to accept a specific theology." It doesn't say "Came to join a certain church or religion."

It says: "Came to believe…" — and leaves the door wide open. This step is about learning to believe that:

- *Healing is possible.*
- *Grace is real.*
- *Something outside yourself is working on your behalf.*
- *You are not alone.*

Progressive Christianity affirms that belief is not about having the "right answers." It's about trusting the right direction — even when the path ahead is foggy. Or even frightening.

Jesus and the Faith of Maybe

One of the most beautiful stories in the Gospels is in Mark 9, where a desperate father brings his suffering child to Jesus and says: "If you can do anything, help us."

Jesus replies, "Everything is possible for the one who believes."

And the father says something that captures the essence of Step Two: "I believe — help my unbelief!"

Jesus doesn't scold him for not having pure faith. He heals anyway. This is what grace looks like: Faith that's mixed with doubt. Hope that feels like a whisper. Belief that's born in exhaustion, not enthusiasm.

Jesus meets people where they are. Step Two invites us to believe that maybe — just maybe, if we embraced Step One and set aside our control — he'll do the same for us.

Keeping in mind that this hope is regardless of how we initially understand Jesus: divine, inspired, prophetic, cosmically kind.

Deconstructing, Rebuilding, and Trusting Again

For many people, especially those coming out of strict or harmful religious environments, Step Two is hard. Believe in what? In whom? After what I've seen? After what I've failed to see?

This step doesn't require you to go back to the God you left. It gives you permission to start fresh — to ask:

- *What kind of God could I trust?*
- *What kind of power would restore, not dominate?*
- *What if Jesus is real, but kinder than I was told?*
- *What if Jesus understood both powerlessness and real spiritual power?*

This isn't about theological perfection. It's about learning to hope again — in something bigger than your own willpower.

God as the Restorer

The word "restore" is key here. It implies:

- *You haven't been destroyed — only damaged.*
- *You're not beyond repair — only in need of care.*
- *You are not starting from scratch — only coming back to who you were made to be.*

- *You can and should have hope — only this time it's grounded in something divine.*

Scripture for Step Two

This is deeply biblical. In the Hebrew scriptures, God is constantly described as a restorer of what's been broken:

"He restores my soul…" (Psalm 23)

"The Lord is close to the brokenhearted and saves those who are crushed in spirit." (Psalm 34)

"I will restore to you the years the locusts have eaten…" (Joel 2:25)

And in the New Testament, Jesus doesn't just forgive — he restores dignity, restores community, restores life itself.

"Yes, we are carrying our own death warrant with us, but it is teaching us not to rely on ourselves, but on a God whose task is to raise the dead to life." (2 Corinthians 1:9)

That's the Higher Power Step Two invites us to imagine: not a punisher, but a repairer, a redirector — a power that can resurrect right here on earth.

Reflection Questions

What does "coming to believe" mean to me right now — not as a final answer, but as a beginning?

What do I want to believe is possible in my recovery?

How would it feel to trust a God who restores, not judges?

What is holding me back from believing in a power greater than myself?

A Step Two Prayer

God of mercy, I want to believe healing is possible.
I'm not sure what I believe about You —
but I know I can't do this alone.
If You are real, meet me where I am.
Restore what's been broken.
Help me trust again — in You, in life, in love.
Help me live again.
Help my disbelief.
Amen.

Chapter 6
Step Three — Turning Over, Not Giving Up
The Surrender That Frees

"Made a decision to turn our will and our lives over to the care of God as we understood Him."
— Step 3 of Alcoholics Anonymous

This is the step people worry about. Turning your life over to God? What does that mean — blind obedience? Religious submission? Losing yourself?

No.

Step Three is not about vanishing. It's about unclenching. Releasing the white knuckles of control and false power. It's the moment in recovery — and in faith — where we stop trying to drive the bus off a cliff and say, "Okay. I'll let love, honesty, compassion and wisdom beyond myself and my ego steer now."

Not because we've given up. But because we're finally ready to loosen our grip, experiment with trust, and be cared for.

A Decision, Not a Drama

Notice what the Step says: "Made a decision…" It doesn't say we had a full spiritual awakening yet. It doesn't say we suddenly trusted God with everything.

It says we decided to begin. To move our hearts and minds in a new direction. This is a pivot — not a leap off a cliff. It's the decision to trust a Higher Power with:

- *Our actions*
- *Our decisions*

- *Our desires*
- *Our plans*
- *Our recovery*
- *Our future*

Not in a way that erases us — but in a way that restores us to ourselves. What Are We Turning Over? Two big things:

1. *Our will* — our impulses, compulsions, selfishness, ego, the need to control outcomes.
2. *Our lives* — our past and future, our identity and purpose, the very shape of our story.

This can be terrifying, unless you truly believe the One you're turning to is good. Not just powerful — good. Not just watching — caring. The genius of this step is the word: "the care of God."

This is not the control of God. This is not the punishment of God. This is care — like a parent cradling a hurting child, or a shepherd tending wounded sheep. To "turn it over" is not to walk away from your human agency. It is to place your life in the hands of a presence that guides and heals.

Jesus and the Will of God

In the Garden of Gethsemane, Jesus utters one of the most honest prayers in Scripture: "Father, if it be your will, take this cup from me. Yet not my will, but yours be done." (Luke 22:42) This is not surrender as spiritual resignation. It is surrender as alignment.

Jesus names what he wants. He's real about his fear. And still — he lets go of control, trusting that God's will is rooted in love and a new kind of strength, not destruction.

A new kind of power revealed in the powerlessness of Step One. That's the kind of surrender Step Three invites. Not a loss of identity, but a deeper trust that the will of God is ultimately for our restoration — not our punishment or ruin.

Letting Go of the Puppet Master

One of the biggest barriers to Step Three is our idea of God. If God is a cosmic micromanager or a divine puppeteer, why would we turn over anything? But if God is:

- *Relational (not robotic)*
- *Loving (not manipulative)*
- *Healing (not controlling)*
- *Liberating (not confining)*

…then surrender looks less like submission and more like coming home.

Progressive Christianity helps reframe this. The will of God isn't a script you have to obey. It's a flow of love, subtle inspiration, and life you learn to trust.

Practical Questions: How Do I Actually "Turn It Over"?

Some simple but profound ways:

- *Begin your day with, "God, guide my thinking, my doing, my being."*
- *In moments of craving or panic, say, "God, I give this to You — just for now."*
- *Imagine God holding your life like a fragile thing — not gripping it, but guarding it.*
- *Keep choosing surrender when control creeps back in (which it will).*

This is not one-and-done. This is daily, hourly, breath-by-breath. That's why it's called a "decision" — not an achievement. A verb, not a noun.

Scripture for Step Three

"Commit your way to the Lord; trust in him, and he will act." (Psalm 37:5)

"Do not be conformed to this world, but be transformed by the renewing of your mind…" (Romans 12:2)

"In him we live and move and have our being." (Acts 17:28)

"Do not be anxious about anything, but in every situation, by prayer and petition, with thanksgiving present your requests to God. And the peace of God, which transcends all understanding, will guard your hearts and minds in Christ Jesus." (Philippians 4:6-7)

Reflection Questions

What parts of my life have I been unwilling to turn over? Why?

What do I think God's "care" looks like?

Where have I seen glimpses of grace when I let go of control?

What does it feel like when I "let go and let God."

A Step Three Prayer

God of gentleness and strength —
I've tried to run things on my own.
I've worn myself out.
Today, I make the decision to trust You —
not just as an idea, but as a loving Presence.
Guide my will. Shape my desires.
Take my life, and hold it in your care.
I'm tired of driving.
Let grace take the wheel.
Take me to a better place.
Amen.

Chapter 7
Step Four — A Searching and Fearless Moral Inventory
Truth Without Shame

"Made a searching and fearless moral inventory of ourselves."
— Step 4 of Alcoholics Anonymous

If you've made it this far, something powerful has already happened:

- *You've admitted there is a problem that's beyond your grasp.*
- *You've begun to believe recovery and healing are possible.*
- *You've chosen to let go of control.*

Or perhaps "share" control as an initial step. Now comes the hard part — and the holy part.

Step Four is where we stop blaming, hiding, or numbing. It's where we name the truth about ourselves — without shame and without shortcuts. It's not about beating yourself up. It's about telling the truth with humility and grace.

The Purpose of Step Four

Let's be clear: Step Four is not a punishment. It's a liberation. We carry so much pain — some of it caused by others, some of it caused by us. But until we name it, we're stuck.

- *Stuck in resentment we never examined.*
- *Stuck in shame we never unpacked.*
- *Stuck in stories we never questioned.*

- *Stuck in a past that has been too hard to examine.*

Step Four is the beginning of emotional and spiritual freedom. It's how we stop running from ourselves and finally start healing from the inside out. It's the start of healthy honesty.

What Makes It "Searching" and "Fearless"?
Searching means we go deeper than surface behavior. We look at motives, patterns, triggers, and fears.

Fearless doesn't mean we feel no fear. It means we're willing to face the fear and move through it.

This step takes courage — not because we're bad, but because we're finally choosing to get honest. And honesty requires bravery, especially when we've built a life around avoiding pain.

The Christian Case for Moral Inventory
This might sound like "confession," and it is — but not the kind loaded with guilt or threat. This is confession as clarity. Scripture is full of people who found God not by being perfect, but by getting real:

- *David wrote "Create in me a clean heart" after owning up to his failures (Psalm 51).*
- *The prodigal son rehearses his confession, only to be embraced before he finishes it.*
- *Jesus says the truth will set us free — not when it's polished, but when it's true.*

Progressive Christianity reframes confession not as humiliation, but as spiritual integrity — an act of courage that returns us to ourselves and to God.

A Gentle Approach to Inventory
Here's what Step Four is not:

- *A list of how awful you are.*
- *A way to relive trauma.*

- *A demand to fix everything immediately.*
  Here's what it is:
- *A mirror held up in grace.*
- *A way to break shame's silence.*
- *A path to understanding yourself without pretending.*

Most people approach Step Four by making a written inventory of:

- *Resentments (who hurt you, what happened, how you responded)*
- *Fears (what drives your reactions, defenses, or silence)*
- *Harms done to others (actions, attitudes, or neglect)*
- *Patterns of behavior (especially those rooted in pain)*
- *And throughout it all: Compassion, Modesty, the critical abandonment of False Pride.*

Jesus and Truth Without Condemnation

One of the most powerful moments in the Gospels is when a woman caught in adultery is dragged before Jesus by angry religious leaders. They want judgment. Jesus kneels in the dust, writes in the sand, and says:

"Let the one without sin cast the first stone." (John 8:7) Then, to the woman, he says: "Neither do I condemn you. Go, and sin no more."

This is the tone of Step Four when done in the light of Christ.

- *Truth without stones.*
- *Honesty without humiliation.*
- *Grace that leads to change, not destruction.*

A Trauma-Informed Note

If your story includes abuse, neglect, or deep trauma: Be kind to yourself. Step Four is not about digging up pain for its own sake. It's about healing, not re-traumatizing. For some, this inventory should be done slowly, with a therapist or sponsor who understands trauma. Honesty is not the same as exposure. Take your time. You are not weak for moving through this step gradually or needing some support.

Scripture for Step Four

"Search me, O God, and know my heart; test me and know my anxious thoughts." (Psalm 139:23)

"…for all that exalt themselves will be humbled, but all who humble themselves will be exalted." (Luke 18:14)

"The light shines on inside the darkness, and the darkness did not overcome it." (John: 1:5)

"If we confess our sins, he is faithful and just to forgive us… and cleanse us from all unrighteousness." (1 John 1:9)

Reflection Questions

What have I avoided telling the truth about — to myself, to God, or to others?

What patterns keep showing up in my life that I haven't fully faced?

How might I approach this inventory with compassion instead of condemnation?

How will it feel to have some of my faults exposed to the light of a loving God?

A Step Four Prayer

Loving God,
I am ready to look within — not to judge, but to heal.
Give me the courage to see clearly.
The gentleness to hold what I find.
The grace to move toward wholeness.
Search me — but not to shame me.

- *A demand to fix everything immediately.*
Here's what it is:
- *A mirror held up in grace.*
- *A way to break shame's silence.*
- *A path to understanding yourself without pretending.*

Most people approach Step Four by making a written inventory of:

- *Resentments (who hurt you, what happened, how you responded)*
- *Fears (what drives your reactions, defenses, or silence)*
- *Harms done to others (actions, attitudes, or neglect)*
- *Patterns of behavior (especially those rooted in pain)*
- *And throughout it all: Compassion, Modesty, the critical abandonment of False Pride.*

Jesus and Truth Without Condemnation

One of the most powerful moments in the Gospels is when a woman caught in adultery is dragged before Jesus by angry religious leaders. They want judgment. Jesus kneels in the dust, writes in the sand, and says:

"Let the one without sin cast the first stone." (John 8:7) Then, to the woman, he says: "Neither do I condemn you. Go, and sin no more."

This is the tone of Step Four when done in the light of Christ.

- *Truth without stones.*
- *Honesty without humiliation.*
- *Grace that leads to change, not destruction.*

A Trauma-Informed Note

If your story includes abuse, neglect, or deep trauma: Be kind to yourself. Step Four is not about digging up pain for its own sake. It's about healing, not re-traumatizing. For some, this inventory should be done slowly, with a therapist or sponsor who understands trauma. Honesty is not the same as exposure. Take your time. You are not weak for moving through this step gradually or needing some support.

Scripture for Step Four

"Search me, O God, and know my heart; test me and know my anxious thoughts." (Psalm 139:23)

"…for all that exalt themselves will be humbled, but all who humble themselves will be exalted." (Luke 18:14)

"The light shines on inside the darkness, and the darkness did not overcome it." (John: 1:5)

"If we confess our sins, he is faithful and just to forgive us… and cleanse us from all unrighteousness." (1 John 1:9)

Reflection Questions

What have I avoided telling the truth about — to myself, to God, or to others?

What patterns keep showing up in my life that I haven't fully faced?

How might I approach this inventory with compassion instead of condemnation?

How will it feel to have some of my faults exposed to the light of a loving God?

A Step Four Prayer

Loving God,
I am ready to look within — not to judge, but to heal.
Give me the courage to see clearly.
The gentleness to hold what I find.
The grace to move toward wholeness.
Search me — but not to shame me.

Search me so that I may be free.
I am ready.
Willing.
Amen

Chapter 8
Step Five — Confession as Freedom
Admitting Our Wrongs to Unbind from Our Past

"Admitted to God, to ourselves, and to another human being the exact nature of our wrongs."
— Step 5 of Alcoholics Anonymous

There are few things harder — or more freeing — than speaking your full truth out loud to another person.

Step Four helped you get honest on paper. Step Five helps you get honest in relationship. This is where secrets lose their power, shame loses its grip, and honesty becomes a sacred bridge — not a solitary burden.

Step Five is not about punishment. It's about freedom and connection.

Why We Speak It Out Loud

If recovery were just an internal process, Step Four would be the end of it. But real healing doesn't happen in isolation. That's why Step Five adds something radical:

- *Speak your truth to God (spiritually)*
- *Speak your truth to yourself (personally)*
- *Speak your truth to another human being (relationally)*
- *Speak your truth to a new more honest future (hopefully)*

This is where recovery becomes communal. Where hiding is transformed into healing. Where accountability meets acceptance.

We speak it out loud so we can stop pretending and stop hiding — not from God, but from ourselves and each other.

The Christian Heart of Confession
In many Christian circles, confession has been turned into either: a shame-drenched ritual or a meaningless habit with no emotional engagement or a plea for supernatural intervention that never seems to happen.

But at its core, confession is about reconnection. In the Bible, confession is rarely about groveling. It's about getting back into right relationship — with God, with others, and with yourself.

- *The Psalmist says: "When I kept silent, my bones wasted away." (Psalm 32:3)*
- *Jesus tells stories where the lost are welcomed before they can even finish confessing.*
- *The early Church practiced confession together, not as punishment, but as a path toward freedom.*
- *Progressive Christianity reclaims confession not as something to be afraid of, but something that leads to grace, healing, and human connection.*

What Does "Exact Nature of Our Wrongs" Mean?
This isn't just a list of bad behaviors. It's about patterns, motives, fears, and deeper truths. For example:

- *Not just "I was angry" — but "I used anger to avoid feeling powerless."*
- *Not just "I lied" — but "I lied because I thought the truth would make me unlovable."*
- *Not just "I hurt someone" — but "I hurt someone because I hadn't yet faced my own pain."*

This step isn't asking for perfection. It's asking for clarity and courage. And the magic happens when someone else hears it — and doesn't flinch. The magic is when you realize you are not alone in your fears and faults.

Choosing the Right Person

This part matters. Step Five isn't about confessing to just anyone. You need:

- *Someone safe*
- *Someone wise*
- *Someone not easily shocked*
- *Someone with clear boundaries*
- *Ideally someone in recovery or trained in pastoral or therapeutic care*

This person is not there to fix you. They are there to hold space for you to own your truth out loud — and survive it. That's what breaks shame's spell.

God Is Not Shocked

Let's be clear: Step Five doesn't inform God of anything new. God already knows. But you might not. You might not remember what honesty sounds and feels like.

Speaking it is not about God learning — it's about you unburdening. The progressive Christian view of God is not a record-keeper of wrongs. It's a presence of love that:

- *Holds our truth with compassion*
- *Desires our healing, not our humiliation*
- *Meets us where we are, not where we should be*
- *Sees our potential, even when it's hidden by faults and failure*

When we confess, we are not trying to earn God's love — we are parting the veil of denial and finally letting it reach us.

Jesus and Shame-Resistant Grace

Think of the woman at the well (John 4). Jesus names her truth — not to shame her, but to set her free. She becomes the first evangelist in the Gospel of John, not because she had it all figured out, but because she was fully seen and still fully loved.

That's what Step Five offers. Not exposure for punishment — but vulnerability for transformation.

Scripture for Step Five

"Therefore confess your sins to one another, and pray for one another, so that you may be healed." (James 5:16)

"When I kept silent, my bones wasted away... Then I acknowledged my sin to you... and you forgave the guilt of my sin." (Psalm 32:3–5)

"I take no pleasure in the death of a wicked man, but in the turning back of a wicked man who changes his ways to win life. Come back, come back!" (Ezekiel: 33:11)

"Neither do I condemn you. Go and sin no more." (John 8:11)

Reflection Questions

What am I most afraid of saying out loud?

Who in my life might be safe enough to hear my full truth?

How are your shames and secrets holding you back from real life?

How does it feel to imagine God hearing my confession with compassion, not condemnation?

A Step Five Prayer

God of truth and tenderness,
I'm ready to speak what I've been hiding.
I'm scared — but I'm willing.

Give me someone who will listen with grace.
Give me the courage to name what's real.
And when I speak, meet me there —
Not to judge, but to heal.
To free me.
To be free.
Amen.

Chapter 9
Step Six — Ready for Change
Warming-up for a Restorative Relationship with God

"Were entirely ready to have God remove all these defects of character."
— Step 6 of Alcoholics Anonymous

After the gut-level honesty of Step Five, Step Six feels quieter. Almost deceptively so. There's no inventory. No confession. No big action.

Just a question: *Am I really ready to change?* Not to perform. Not to impress. But to be transformed — from the inside out.

Step Six is where we face our resistance, our fears, and our defenses. It's where we stop trying to self-improve and start learning to cooperate with grace.

The Misunderstood Word: "Defects of Character"

Let's deal with the language. "Defects" can sound harsh, even shaming. But what AA means here isn't that you're broken or worthless — it's that some of your habits, behaviors, fears, and coping strategies are no longer serving your healing and sobriety.

In a progressive Christian frame, you are not defective. You are wounded, and some of your patterns — even if they once protected you — are now harming you or others.

This step isn't about getting rid of who you are. It's about letting go of what no longer belongs in the new life you're building.

Entirely Ready?

Step Six adds the word entirely, and it's a big one. It doesn't mean you're flawless in your intentions. It means:

- *You've stopped defending your old patterns.*
- *You've stopped pretending your rage, pride, fear, control, or avoidance are "just how I am."*
- *You're willing — not able, willing — to let grace, trust, and the new network you are building around you, do work you cannot do on your own.*

Readiness doesn't mean you're fearless. It means you're done with the old way.

What Step Six Is Not

- *It is not the removal of character defects themselves (that's Step Seven).*
- *It is not a demand to be instantly free from all struggles.*
- *It is not a guilt-trip for not being better already.*
- *It's not walking away from your agency.*

This step simply asks: Are you willing to let God change you in the places that scare you, shame you, or seem too tangled up to touch? If the answer is "yes," even with trembling hands and some fear of what it all means — you're ready.

The Jesus Way: Grace Before Change

One of the great misconceptions in Christianity is that change precedes grace — that God helps those who help themselves, or that we must clean up before showing up.

But in the Gospels, it's always the other way around:

- *Zacchaeus is invited before he repents.*
- *The woman caught in adultery is forgiven before she changes.*
- *Peter is restored before he proves himself.*

In Step Six, you're not fixing yourself for God. You're finally letting God meet you where change is most needed — and most feared.

This is transformation by proximity, not pressure. Said differently, willingness is opening the door and letting grace come into your life — whether you think you are ready or not.

God as Co-Creator, Not Fixer

In progressive theology, God doesn't swoop in to erase your personality or overwrite your will. God is not magical Genie who grants wishes left and right. Instead, God partners with your willingness to create something new. It's not "zap!" It's more like:

- *Unfolding*
- *Pruning*
- *Refashioning*
- *Reorienting*

Think of God as a potter (Jeremiah 18), reshaping clay that's already good — but needs to be softened, re-wetted, reworked. You are not being discarded; You are being formed.

When You're Not Entirely Ready

Sometimes we're only partly ready. That's okay too. Many people pray: "God, make me willing to be willing."

This, too, is enough. Grace meets you at the point of your desire, not your perfection. Even naming your reluctance is a sacred act. "I'm not sure. But I'm willing." That's progress.

Scripture for Step Six

"Create in me a clean heart, O God, and renew a right spirit within me." (Psalm 51:10)

"Behold, I am making all things new." (Revelation 21:5)

"We are God's workmanship, created in Christ Jesus for good works…" (Ephesians 2:10)

"This is what I shall tell my heart, and so recover hope: the favors of Yahweh are not all passed, his kindnesses are not exhausted. They are renewed every morning." (Lamentations 3:21-22)

Reflection Questions

What patterns or traits have I tried to change but can't seem to change on my own?

What am I still holding onto — even if it's hurting me?

Do I have "defects of character" that give me a false sense of strength?

How do I imagine God partnering with me in transformation?

How can I God working if God works slowly over time without "zaps" and quick fixes?

What does partnership with God mean in the life that I lead?

A Step Six Prayer

God of mercy and movement,
I've named what's hurting me — and others.
Now I want to be free.
I'm not asking for perfection.
I'm asking for willingness.
Make me ready, God.
Ready to release what clings to me.

*Ready to release what I cling to.
I'm ready to trust that grace can reshape what I cannot.
Trust in my imperfect trust.
Amen.*

Chapter 10
Step Seven — Humbly Asked God
A Partnership in Transformation

"Humbly asked Him to remove our shortcomings."
— Step 7 of Alcoholics Anonymous

Step Six was about getting ready. Step Seven is about asking. But this isn't a magic formula or a last-ditch Hail Mary. This is a prayer born out of relationship. It's not just asking to be changed — it's trusting the One who changes us.

This step moves us from admission to participation — not through striving, but through humility and hope.

What Does "Humbly" Mean?

The word humble often gets confused with humiliation. That's not what this step is about. To be humble means:

- *To be grounded in reality.*
- *To be open to help.*
- *To stop pretending you're the center of the universe.*
- *To see your value without inflating your ego.*

It's the posture of someone who knows they can't do it all alone — and also knows they are worthy of transformation. Humility is not about thinking less of yourself. It's about thinking truthfully about yourself — and trusting that grace will meet you in that truth.

Why Ask God?

Because transformation isn't just behavior modification. It's soul-level change — the kind we can't manufacture on our own. When we ask God to remove our shortcomings, we're saying: "I've done all I can do. Now I surrender what I can't."

This step is not a resignation. It's a collaboration. You've done the inventory. You've admitted your patterns. You've opened your hands. Now you let God work — not around you, but within you.

The Progressive Christian Vision of Divine Change

In a progressive faith context, we don't see God as a supernatural fixer who chooses winners and losers, snaps fingers and zaps away problems and flaws. Instead, we see a God who:

- *Moves through relationship, not force.*
- *Honors your consent and quietly inspires your agency.*
- *Understands the context of your life, including your family and history.*
- *Works slowly and deeply, like yeast in dough or a seed in soil. (Matthew 13)*

God doesn't erase your personality. God refines your character. Not by changing who you are, but by healing the parts twisted by fear, trauma, and ego. This is not self-improvement. This is subtle, sacred transformation – positive evolution.

The Role of Prayer in Transformation

Prayer is not about informing God. It's about inviting God. It's not about performing worthiness. It's about practicing willingness.

When we pray in Step Seven, we're not asking for a miracle or some kind of personality transfusion.

We're saying: "God, help me become the person You've been calling me to be all along."

It's okay if the prayer is simple. It's okay if it's clumsy. It just needs to be honest. Even "Help." is a holy word in this step. In fact, "help me" may be the first sound of Step Seven.

Jesus, Humility, and Transformation

In Philippians 2, we're told that Jesus "humbled himself… even to death on a cross." That's the humility we're invited into — not self-hate, but self-giving love. Surely this is too radical an example for a mere mortal trying to get clen and sober.

But this is what happens next in that story: "Therefore God highly exalted him…" You see, Step Seven is following a divine pattern:

- *We descend in honesty.*
- *We ask in humility.*
- *And we are lifted by grace.*

And in our case, we are lifted, not to greatness, but to wholeness. Human wholeness being the goal all along.

What If Nothing Changes Right Away?

Step Seven isn't always flashy. Sometimes the "removal" of shortcomings looks like:

- *A pause before reacting.*
- *A moment of clarity before old behavior takes over.*
- *A growing discomfort with old patterns.*
- *A deeper compassion for your own triggers.*

Sometimes it's one day of peace in a week of chaos. Sometimes it's simply this: This time you didn't give up or give in or go backwards. You held steady. That's change. That's grace in motion.

Scripture for Step Seven

"He has shown you, O mortal, what is good… to do justice, love mercy, and walk humbly with your God." (Micah 6:8)

"Have mercy on me, O God, in your goodness, in your great tenderness wipe away all my faults, wash me clean of my guilt, and purify me from all my sin." (Psalm 51:1-2)

"The one who began a good work in you will carry it on to completion…" (Philippians 1:6)

Reflection Questions

What shortcomings am I truly ready to have removed?

What would my life look like without the self-destructive parts of my own ego?

Which shortcomings are strongly protected by my ego?

Where do I see God already at work reshaping me?

What does humility look like in my life right now?

A Step Seven Prayer

God please hear me.
I've tried to fix myself — and failed.
Now I come with open hands.
Remove what keeps me from wholeness.
Heal what I cannot reach.
I am not asking to be perfect.
I am asking to be free of my own failings.
I trust that You are already at work.

Help me be a partner in my salvation.
Make me new — gently, truthfully, and fully.
See my humility.
Amen.

Chapter 11
Step Eight — Making the List
Facing the People We've Hurt with Courage and Care

"Made a list of all persons we had harmed, and became willing to make amends to them all."
— Step 8 of Alcoholics Anonymous

By now, you've told the truth to yourself. You've admitted it to God and another person. You've begun to hand over what you can't fix on your own. Now, the focus shifts outward: to those you've harmed.

Step Eight is the beginning of relational restoration. It doesn't ask you to make amends yet. It asks you to face the truth of your impact, and to open your heart and your mind to making things right. This step is about courage, clarity, and — most of all — honest, ethical readiness.

The Two Parts of Step Eight
There's a beautiful rhythm to this step: Make a list — This is about being thorough, not selective. Become willing — This is about being honest with your fear and resistance, and asking for the clear-eyed inner strength to move forward anyway.

This isn't a list of your feelings. It's a list of your impact — regardless of your intentions. And that's what makes this step so powerful — and so uncomfortable.

Harm vs. Hurt Feelings
In recovery — and in life — it's easy to confuse disagreement or misunderstanding with actual harm.

Step Eight invites you to reflect deeper. It asks you to think seriously about how you affected people in your life. Harm includes:

- *Lying*
- *Manipulating*
- *Betraying trust*
- *Abandoning*
- *Using people*
- *Stealing, physically or emotionally*
- *Inflicting emotional, spiritual, or physical pain*

Not all harm was malicious. Not all harm was recent. But all of it matters. Step Eight says: Name it. List it. Face it. Not to wallow in shame — but to make room for restoration.

What About the People Who Hurt Me?

This step isn't about them. That comes later, when we'll talk about boundaries, mutual healing, and what it means to forgive, or not forgive. For now, the focus is your side of the street. This isn't a step about blame — it's a step about ownership.

The Theology of Making Things Right

In the Gospels, Jesus teaches that love for God is inseparable from love for neighbor — especially the neighbor you've wronged.

"So when you are offering your gift at the altar, if you remember that your brother or sister has something against you, leave you gift there before the alter and go; first be reconciled to your brother or sister, and then come and offer your gift." — Matthew 5:23–24

Jesus doesn't say, "Be ashamed."
He says, "Be restored."

Progressive Christianity adds this: We believe healing isn't just personal — it's relational and social. We confess not to be crushed, but to be reconnected. We seek justice — not to punish, but to repair.

Becoming Willing

Many people can make a list. Few are immediately willing to follow through. That's okay. The step doesn't demand instant action. It asks for a posture of readiness:

- *Ready to name what happened.*
- *Ready to be humbled.*
- *Ready to consider how apology and amends might be possible — even if it's complicated.*
- *Ready to confront our past from a very personal perspective.*

Willingness might not feel strong. It might feel like an intuition. A distant desire to make things right. That's the beginning. That's enough.

When It Still Feels Like Too Much

You might think:

- *"They don't want to hear from me."*
- *"I'll just make it worse."*
- *"It's been too long."*
- *"I already apologized."*
- *"They hurt me too."*

These are real fears. And some may even be valid concerns. But Step Eight doesn't ask you to act yet. It simply says: Make the list. The list is like opening the door.

The how and when comes in Step Nine. This is inner preparation for outer repair.

Scripture for Step Eight

"Let each of you look not to your own interests, but to the interests of others." (Philippians 2:4)

"Do to others as you would have them do to you." (Luke 6:31)

"Restore them gently… and carry each other's burdens." (Galatians 6:1–2)

"Therefore confess your sins to one another, and pray for one another, so that you may be healed." (James 5:16)

Reflection Questions

Who have I harmed — through actions, neglect, or words?

What would it mean to be willing to make things right, even if I don't yet know how?

What holds me back from willingness — and can I bring that fear to God?

How have the previous steps prepared me for this moment?

A Step Eight Prayer

God of restoration,
I've hurt others in my addiction.
I want to face the truth — not to shame myself, but to heal.
Help me make the list.
Help me face my past.
I trust that You desire wholeness — not just in me, but in the people around me.
Give me courage, humility, and the heart of a peacemaker.
Amen.

Chapter 12
Step Nine — Making Amends
Healing Without Expectation, Relationships Without Control

"Made direct amends to such people wherever possible, except when to do so would injure them or others."
— Step 9 of Alcoholics Anonymous

This is the step where things get real. You've looked inward. You've admitted your truth. You've opened your heart, mind and pride to transformation. Now, you begin the slow, holy work of repair.

Step Nine is not about undoing the past. It's about honoring the people affected by it. It's not about groveling or begging forgiveness. It's about showing up in love, honesty, and humility — and letting the other person respond however they choose.

You're not here to control the outcome. You're here to make space for healing — even if that healing takes place in them, not with them.

What Amends Are — and Are Not
Let's clarify. Amends are:

- *Direct efforts to make things right*
- *Honest, humble acknowledgments of harm*
- *Respectful of the other person's readiness, boundaries, and safety*
- *Centered in your responsibility — not their response*

Amends are not:

- *Forced apologies*
- *A way to earn forgiveness*

- *An emotional dumping ground*
- *A shortcut to avoid guilt*
- *A demand for reconciliation*

This step isn't about getting anything for yourself. It's about giving something back — dignity, clarity, ownership, peace.

Jesus and the Ministry of Repair

One of the clearest biblical models of amends is Zacchaeus — the greedy tax collector in Luke 19 who climbs a tree to see Jesus. When Jesus encounters him, he doesn't preach against his greed. He simply invites himself to the house of Zacchaeus, a man the people consider a sinner.

And Zacchaeus, moved by that presence, says: "If I have defrauded anyone, I will repay it four times as much." Jesus replies: "Today salvation has come to this house." Zacchaeus doesn't earn grace by making amends — he makes amends because he's already encountered it. The grace shown by Jesus gave him a new kind of trust.

That's the posture of Step Nine: You're not earning forgiveness. You're living out the restoration of your relationships, and the new freedom of your own life.

When Amends Might Cause Harm

The step includes a vital qualifier: "...except when to do so would injure them or others." Sometimes direct amends would:

- *Reopen old wounds*
- *Force unwanted contact*
- *Violate a boundary*
- *Cause trauma or confusion*
- *Burden someone who's not ready*
- *Serve you more than it serves them*

In those cases, indirect amends may be more appropriate — a heartfelt letter never sent, a donation in a person's name, and most importantly living differently going forward, knowing that healthy relationships in the future are the very spirit of amends for the past.

Regardless of the action taken, discernment matters here. Talk to a sponsor, therapist, or spiritual advisor before acting. Amends are not about your relief — they're about the other person's dignity and safety.

Letting Go of the Outcome

This step requires you to release control. You may:

- *Not be forgiven*
- *Not be acknowledged*
- *Not get closure*
- *Not sense relief*

That's okay. The spiritual act is not in how they respond — but in your readiness to offer healing without strings attached.

In a progressive Christian lens, this is *kenosis* — self-emptying love, the kind Christ shows in Philippians 2. It's love without manipulation, without entitlement, without demand.

When Amends Are Received with Grace

Sometimes, a moment of profound reconciliation happens. Tears fall. Old pain is released. A relationship is restored.

A shared sense of relief defines the moment and speaks to the future. These moments are gifts — sacred glimpses of what grace can do. But they are grace, not guarantee. Cherish them, but don't chase them.

Scripture for Step Nine

"If possible, so far as it depends on you, live peaceably with all." (Romans 12:18)

"Blessed are the peacemakers, for they will be called children of God." (Matthew 5:9)

"Let us love not in word or speech but in truth and action." (1 John 3:18)

"Let each of you look not to your own interests, but to the interests of others." (Philippians 2:4)

Reflection Questions

Where in my life is an amends still needed?

How can I approach this person with humility, not pressure?

Have I really sought to understand how damaging my actions have been to other people?

Am I willing to offer healing even if I'm not received with open arms?

Am I willing to be truly vulnerable with the people I have wronged?

Is my motivation truly for the good of the other?

Could I handle rejection with grace and understanding?

A Step Nine Prayer

God of reconciliation and mercy.
I want to make things right.
Not to erase the past —
but to honor those I've hurt and to live differently going forward.
Give me courage.
Give me compassion.
Help me release control of the outcome.

Teach me to love without expectation.
And let healing flow, even if I never see it bloom.
Amen.

Chapter 13
Step Ten — Daily Cleaning
Staying Honest One Day at a Time

"Continued to take personal inventory and when we were wrong promptly admitted it."
— Step 10 of Alcoholics Anonymous

By now, you've come to understand the process of deep work and real introspection. You've looked at your past. You've begun to make amends. You've surrendered and been reshaped. Finally, the future can be faced with honest optimism.

Step Ten is how you keep this freedom, courage and conviction alive and active in your daily life. This is the step that says: "Let's not wait until things fall apart again. Let's keep it clean — one day at a time."

Not perfectly. Not obsessively. But with presence, self-awareness, and the humility to course-correct early.

Recovery Is Maintenance, Not Perfection
Step Ten is like spiritual hygiene. Just as you wouldn't wait to brush your teeth, this step invites you to keep accurate accounts with yourself, others, and God. It's about maintaining spiritual health.

It's not about avoiding all mistakes — it's about responding quickly, honestly and appropriately when they happen. This is the daily spiritual rhythm of:
- *Pausing*
- *Reviewing*
- *Admitting*

- *Realigning*

No drama. No hiding. Just a steady walk in the life of an always growing, always maturing adult.

What Does a Daily Inventory Look Like?

There's no one-size-fits-all method, but here are common questions people use for a quick end-of-day review:

- *Where was I resentful, fearful, or dishonest today?*
- *Did I hurt anyone — with words, silence, attitude, or action?*
- *Did I avoid responsibility, project blame, or manipulate?*
- *Was I kind to myself and others?*
- *Where did I see grace today?*

You don't need to beat yourself up. You're not writing an indictment — just checking in. If something needs amending, make it. If something needs releasing, let it go. If something went well, celebrate that too.

Promptly Admitted It

That word "promptly" matters. The longer we wait to admit our wrongs, the heavier they get. Resentments build. Defensiveness creeps in. Relationships suffer.

Step Ten invites you to keep your side of the street clean in real time, or as soon as you're aware of the mess. There is no time for denial or defensiveness. This is grace in motion — not reactive guilt, but proactive honesty.

Jesus and the Practice of Self-Examination

Jesus constantly invites people to look within — not with shame, but with compassionate clarity. In Matthew 7, he says: "Take the log out of your own eye first..." A metaphor for blindness to our own shortcomings.

This isn't about self-criticism — it's about clear vision. When we examine ourselves humbly, we see others more graciously.

And in John 13, Jesus models daily cleansing when he washes his disciples' feet — not because they were covered in mud, but because they had walked through their own experience of trials and temptations.

Step Ten is the same. You're not evil. You're dusty. And that's what daily grace is for. The divine discipline of clean living.

A Progressive Christian Lens on Ongoing Change

Transformation is not a moment. It's a movement — and it requires ongoing participation and engagement with the joys and challenges of life.

Progressive Christianity understands sanctification not as moral perfection, but as a lifelong unfolding of awareness and soulful evolution. This step is the daily practice of becoming who you already are in Christ — a beloved, growing, grace-shaped person.

Avoiding the Pitfalls
Obsession vs. Apathy

This step can go off track in two ways:

- *Obsession:* You become hyper-critical, reviewing every moment with anxiety. This is not the Spirit of Step Ten.
- *Apathy:* You drift away from self-examination, letting small things build up until they become big things.

The middle way is ongoing awareness. Honest curiosity. Loving correction. This step doesn't ask you to be anxious — it asks you to stay awake.

Scripture for Step Ten

"Search me, O God, and know my heart… See if there is any wicked way in me, and lead me in the way everlasting." (Psalm 139:23-24)

"Let anyone who thinks they are standing take heed, lest they fall." (1 Corinthians 10:12)

"Create in me a clean heart, O God, and renew a right spirit within me." (Psalm 51:10)

"Even pagans who never heard of the law, can be said to 'be' the law; it is engraved on their hearts. They can call forth this witness, their own inner mental dialogue of accusation and defense." (Romans 2:14-15)

Reflection Questions

What did I learn about myself today?

Was there anything I need to admit — to God, to another person, or to myself?

How can I approach daily inventory with integrity, not fear?

Can I hear my own self critic as honest, not harmful?

A Step Ten Prayer

God of every ordinary day,
I want to stay close to the truth.
Not out of fear — but because freedom is found in honesty.
Search me gently.
Show me what I need to see.
Help me admit what's mine without shame or delay.
Keep my heart clean,
my relationships honest,
and my soul awake.
Amen.

Chapter 14
Step Eleven — Conscious Contact
Prayer, Presence, and the Daily Dance with God

"Sought through prayer and meditation to improve our conscious contact with God as we understood Him, praying only for knowledge of His will for us and the power to carry that out."
— *Step 11 of Alcoholics Anonymous*

If Step Ten helps us stay honest, Step Eleven helps us stay connected to the source of our honesty. By now, you've begun to think about and experience the presence of a Higher Power — perhaps for the first time, or perhaps in a new and deeper way.

Step Eleven invites you to nurture that experience and relationship — not through ritual or performance, but through attention, intention and intimacy. This step is the heartbeat of spiritual life in recovery.

You can call it your spiritual practice. It's not about "being religious." It's about keeping self-will balanced between your powerlessness and higher power — one day at a time.

What Is Conscious Contact?

It's one thing to believe in God. It's another thing to live aware of God's presence. That's what "conscious contact" means:

- *Bringing God into the moment.*
- *Learning to listen, not just speak.*
- *Paying attention to love, nudges, convictions, and quiet wisdom.*

- *Practicing awareness in daily life — not just in crisis.*
- *Taking time to make decisions — being patient.*

This isn't about proving you're spiritual. It's about staying spiritually engaged and aware.

Prayer and Meditation — Together

AA's *Big Book* wisely pairs these practices.
Prayer is speaking to God — in gratitude, need, confession, or desire. Meditation is listening — resting in silence, breathing deeply, watching your thoughts, or simply being with God.

You don't have to sit cross-legged or light incense. You just need a willingness to pause, open, and be. Instead of being reactive, you are being inter-active with your higher power.

In progressive Christianity, this is often called spiritual or contemplative practice — the ancient rhythm of stillness and communion with the Divine.

Jesus and the Rhythm of Prayer

Jesus constantly sought solitude to pray:

- *In the morning (Mark 1:35)*
- *Before major decisions (Luke 6:12)*
- *In grief (Matthew 14:13)*
- *In anxiety (Luke 22:41–44)*

He didn't pray to impress anyone. He prayed to stay aligned with God — to ground himself in love, clarity, and courage. This is what Step Eleven invites us into:

- *Not performance, but presence.*
- *Not magical thinking, but meaningful connection.*
- *Not creeds and formulas, but friendship with and trust in God.*

Knowledge of God's Will — Not Control, but the Lure of Wisdom

Notice what the Step says we're praying for: "Knowledge of God's will for us and the power to carry it out."

This isn't about figuring out a master plan or asking God to micromanage our lives. It's about discernment — being led by morality, guided by purpose, and empowered by the greater good. God's will is not a rigid path — it's a flow of mercy, justice, peace and truth that we're invited to join.

In this step, we're not asking, "God, tell me every next move," but rather, "God, show me the next right thing. Help me see clearly. Then help me make choices and take action with a clean heart."

Prayer and Meditation in Everyday Life

Prayer doesn't have to be fancy. Try this:

- *"God, be with me today."*
- *"Guide my thinking, my words, my actions."*
- *"Help me see You in others."*
- *"Remind me I'm not alone."*
- *"Show me how to love."*
- *"Please help keep me centered."*

Meditation can be simple, too:

- *Sit in silence for five minutes and breathe deeply.*
- *Repeat a sacred word or verse slowly: "Be still and know"*
- *Pay attention to your heartbeat.*
- *Quietly watch the plants and animals around you.*
- *Practice "welcoming prayer": "God, I welcome Your presence in this moment."*
- *Visualize a calm or beautiful place in nature.*

Spirituality doesn't have to be loud or complicated to be influential and alive.

Progressive Christianity and a Listening Faith

Progressive Christianity embraces mystery. It knows that God is often quiet, or simply waits with us. We don't need absolute certainty to pray. We don't need a script to meditate. We don't need to feel spiritual to stay spiritually connected.

What matters is desire, openness — and attention. This step is a call back to the sacred center where God already dwells.

Scripture for Step Eleven

"Be still and know that I am God." (Psalm 46:10)

"Pray without ceasing." (1 Thessalonians 5:17)

"The Spirit helps us in our weakness... intercedes with groans too deep for words." (Romans 8:26)

"You must put aside your old self which has been corrupted by following illusory desires. Your mind must be renewed by a spiritual revolution." (Ephesians 4:22-23)

Reflection Questions

When do I feel most connected to God — or to something greater?

What kind of prayer or meditation resonates most with me?

How can I make conscious contact a common, daily habit?

Where do I feel the inspiration of my higher power?

A Step Eleven Prayer

God of presence and peace,
I want to stay connected.
Not just when things fall apart,
but in the quiet, in the ordinary, in the in-between.
Teach me to listen.

Teach me to breathe.
Help me seek You with honesty — and hear You without fear.
Show me Your will.
Strengthen me to follow it.
Let this day be shaped by love.
Amen.

Chapter 15
Step Twelve — The Awakening
Carrying the Message and Living the Grace

"Having had a spiritual awakening as the result of these steps, we tried to carry this message to alcoholics, and to practice these principles in all our affairs."
— Step 12 of Alcoholics Anonymous

This is where everything comes full circle. Not because you've arrived — but because you are awake, aware and truly present. You've experienced something real. You've faced your pain, experienced truth, reached for God, and begun to live in new ways.

Now, you don't just hold this thing called grace — you share it. Step Twelve is the spiritual call to give away what you've received. Not to fix people. Not to be anyone's hero. But to show up, listen, reflect the truth, and walk with others the way someone walked with you.

What Is a "Spiritual Awakening"?

It's not a lightning bolt. It's not enlightenment on demand. It's not the end of struggle. A spiritual awakening is:

- *Clarity where there used to be chaos.*
- *Connection where there used to be isolation.*
- *Purpose where there used to be aimless drifting.*
- *Willingness where there used to be denial.*
- *Peace where there used to be panic.*

It's the growing awareness that you are not alone, and that grace has power — something very different than the power we gave up in Step One.

Awakening means you see life differently — not perfectly, but with a new kind of vision. And that vision changes how you act and live in the real world.

Carrying the Message

This doesn't mean preaching. It doesn't mean pushing. It doesn't mean having all the answers.

- *It means sharing your story.*
- *It means showing up with humility.*
- *It means letting your recovery be visible — not to impress, but to inspire honesty and hope.*

In progressive Christian terms, this is incarnational living: letting the grace that has transformed you take shape in your daily actions, words, and presence.

It's giving your faith "feet" so it can walk out into the world as both an advocate and inspiration for other addicts. You become the message — not by being perfect, but by showing up and being real.

Practice These Principles in All Our Affairs

This line brings it home: Recovery isn't just for the meeting. Spirituality isn't just for Sunday. Faith isn't just for your journal or your step work.

Step Twelve asks: How can I live these principles — surrender, truth-telling, amends, grace, presence — in my relationships, my work, my community, and an outer reflection of my inner life? You won't do it perfectly. But you can do it earnestly. The result?

- *A life of integrity.*
- *A life of service.*
- *A life of growing freedom.*

Jesus: The Embodied Twelve Stepper

Jesus didn't sit in a temple waiting for the "spiritually ready" to show up. He went to the streets. The margins. The hurting. The shamed. The outcasts. He told the truth.

He modeled surrender. He lived in alignment with God's will. He made amends in action. He carried a message — and became the message. And then he passed it on: "Go and do likewise."

That's Step Twelve: Not preaching about grace — living it out loud.

You're Not Done. You're Living.

Step Twelve isn't a graduation. It's the beginning of ongoing practice. A spiritual rhythm of:

- *Continuing the steps.*
- *Reaching out to the newcomer.*
- *Sharing our strength hope and experience.*
- *Encouraging progress rather than perfection.*
- *Keeping sight of where our journey started.*

The message you carry isn't "look at how far I've come." It's "you're not alone, and you don't have to stay stuck." That's resurrection. That's recovery. That's seeing the world as the Body of Christ.

Scripture for Step Twelve

"What was given to your freely, you must give away freely." (Matthew 10:8)

"Let your light shine before others…" (Matthew 5:16)

"Bear one another's burdens, and in this way you fulfill the law of Christ." (Galatians 6:2)

"Simon, Simon, you must be sifted like wheat, and once you have recovered, you in your turn must strengthen your brothers." (Luke 22:31-32)

Reflection Questions

What does my "spiritual awakening" look like right now?

What does it feel like – in good times, and bad?

Who can I walk with, listen to, or encourage?

How will I know if I'm not "practicing these principles"?

A Step Twelve Prayer

God of every step –
I've been held.
I've been healed.
And now I want to live in a way that honors what You've done in me.
Let my story be honest.
Let my presence be kind.
Let my life be a message of grace in motion.
Show me who needs to know they're not alone.
Let me carry light – not perfection, but peace.
And when I forget, bring me back.
Again and again.
Amen.

Epilogue to Part II
The Steps Are a Spiral, Not a Straight Line

You will walk these steps more than once. That's not failure. That's faithfulness. It's your commitment to a growing spirituality and a constantly evolving life. It's what we are here for.

Progressive Christianity — like recovery — is not about arrival. It's about returning: to God, to truth, to grace, and to each other. You're not done. You're alive. And you're not walking alone.

Part III
Living Grace Forward in Progressive Recovery

Chapter 16
When God Still Feels Complicated

"Now we see in a mirror, dimly..." — 1 Corinthians 13:12

Even after working the steps, making amends, and practicing prayer and meditation more regularly, many people still wrestle with their image of God. And that's okay. The wrestling — the searching — is part of the growth. It leads us to new revelations.

Spiritual clarity doesn't usually arrive at Step Twelve like a lightning bolt. For many, recovery clarifies behavior and relationships, and the process itself can be the platform for belief. Faith in the process, belief in the outcomes. This chapter is a permission slip for anyone who still feels uneasy about:

- *The God of their childhood.*
- *The language of "Him."*
- *The silence that sometimes follows prayer.*
- *The theological baggage of religion.*
- *The mystery that never seems to fully resolve.*
- *The suffering that happens in this unperfect world.*

God Is Not a Test You Have to Pass

Recovery doesn't require orthodoxy. It requires honesty. And remember, creeds are man-made, not God-given. Progressive Christianity understands that you take what you need and leave the rest.

If your understanding of God still feels incomplete, you're in good company — Moses didn't get a full picture. The apostle Paul admitted his knowledge was partial. Even Jesus cried out, "Why have you forsaken me?"

Step Eleven wasn't a demand to feel God, only to seek conscious contact. Step Twelve didn't ask for spiritual certainty — only that you carry the divine inspiration and intuition you've received. You don't have to understand God to be transformed by grace.

Faith as a Long Conversation

Progressive Christianity honors the idea that faith evolves:

- *The names we use for God change.*
- *The images that once wounded us lose power.*
- *The metaphors that once confused us become meaningful.*
- *The doubts that haunted us become doorways.*
- *The fear of divine punishment slips away.*

Recovery doesn't erase theological tension or answer all questions about God. It just teaches you how to live in this world without shame and embrace questions with openness and healthy curiosity.

Your walk with God is not a closed book. It's a living conversation. Keep listening. Keep asking. Keep walking.

Chapter 17
Beyond Belief
A Faith That Acts

"Faith without works is dead." — James 2:17

Having a spiritual awakening doesn't mean becoming spiritually passive. Rather, the very act and process of recovery can become an entirely honest and organic Christian witness.

One of the gifts of recovery is that it teaches us that faith is embodied — not just in beliefs, but in behavior:

- *Making amends becomes a form of justice.*
- *Sponsoring others becomes a ministry.*
- *Showing up at meetings becomes a sacred discipline.*
- *Serving, forgiving, speaking truth — these become like worship.*

In short, the 12 Steps help us to practice recovery principles in ways that reflect the justice and love of Christ:

- *Advocating for those in addiction and poverty.*
- *Healing family systems scarred by secrecy and shame.*
- *Naming and challenging injustice without losing compassion.*
- *Living out spiritual maturity through kindness, boundaries, and presence.*

The Sermon on the Mount as the Spiritual Awakening in Action

Jesus' teaching in Matthew 5–7 sounds a lot like Step Twelve:

- *Blessed are the poor in spirit*
- *Blessed are the merciful*
- *Turn the other cheek*
- *Do unto others*
- *Let your yes be yes*
- *Love your enemy*
- *Don't judge*
- *Seek first the kingdom of God*

These aren't rules to earn grace — they're responses to what may now feel like a divine presence. They're how people who have been changed by love begin to love in return. Recovery doesn't just give you clarity. It gives you a calling.

Chapter 18
Creating Communities of Healing

"They devoted themselves to the apostles' teaching and to fellowship... and all who believed were together and had all things in common." — Acts 2:42, 44

The early church wasn't built on creeds and belief statements — it was built on fellowship, vulnerability, confession, service, and mercy. Sound familiar?

The church and the recovery group share a holy overlap — when they're at their best, they are places where people:

- *Tell the truth*
- *Find belonging*
- *Confess without fear*
- *Serve without ego*
- *Grow without shame*
- *Return again and again*

For some people, a progressive Christian approach to addiction is also an invitation to become bridge-builders between recovery and faith communities:

- *Helping churches learn from the humility of 12-step culture.*
- *Building small groups that prioritize honesty over performance.*
- *Supporting spiritual seekers with no religious background.*
- *Making recovery spaces more accessible to people who long for spiritual language but not spiritual control.*

- *Honestly addressing the damage that can be done by religious language.*

You Are a Living Invitation

You don't have to start a ministry to create a healing space. You just have to keep doing what you're already doing:

- *Listening with love*
- *Speaking without shame*
- *Showing up in truth*
- *Sharing what's helped you*
- *Staying in the process — visibly*
- *You are the bridge. You are the witness.*
- *You are living proof that grace still works.*

Final Word
Higher Power in Every Step

You don't need to go back to the beginning to keep growing. You just need to keep moving — one honest, surrendered, grace-filled step at a time. This short book is not a conclusion. It's a companion.

The steps will spiral back — deeper each time. Your understanding of God may shift again. The people you help will also help you. And your life, in all its imperfection, can become a sacred witness.

- *You are not perfect.*
- *You are not done.*
- *You are not alone.*
- *You are loved.*
- *You are healing.*
- *You are living grace forward.*

Part IV
Theological Reflections on the 12 Steps

Chapter 19
Why Theology Matters in Recovery

Recovery is not just physical or emotional work. It is deeply spiritual work as we've come to understand in the previous pages. Journeying through the 12 Steps, we inevitably ask — and often re-ask — spiritual questions: Who or what is the "Power greater than ourselves"? What is the nature of grace? How does healing happen, and what does God have to do with it?

For many people shaped by Christianity — whether traditional, progressive, or evolving in their faith and understanding — theological assumptions shape how they engage these questions. Some carry images of God as an all-powerful ruler, expecting submission, obedience and even supernatural intervention. Others hold to visions of God as loving, relational, and dynamically involved in a person's growth and evolution — their "human becoming."

This section offers brief, introductory reflections to help readers thoughtfully engage the spiritual layers of the 12 Steps through different lenses. Here, we explore how various theological approaches — Traditional Christianity, Progressive Christianity, Process Theology, and Open-and-Relational Theology — interpret and illuminate the recovery journey.

In the following pages Traditional and Progressive Christianity are compared and contrasted in relation to each of the 12 Steps, and Process Theology and Open-and-Relational Theology are applied to the steps individually, as their similarities are strong and their differences are subtle.

The goal is to help you find a theology that speaks to your soul, inspires further study and helps to guide you on your recovery path. This is about your journey and your higher power. "God" is a word that can be understood and experienced from many perspectives.

Traditional and Progressive Christianity on the 12 Steps

Different expressions of Christianity shape how people engage with the 12 Steps. This section explores how traditional interpretations — often rooted in doctrines of sin, submission, divine authority and biblical literalism — contrast with progressive interpretations that emphasize love, relationality, grace and a more metaphorical interpretation of scripture. These differences profoundly shape how we experience surrender, confession, and spiritual growth in recovery.

Process Theology and the 12 Steps

Process Theology offers a dynamic and compassionate vision of God as persuasive rather than coercive, relational rather than detached. This section explores an understanding of God as optimistically involved in our lives and oriented towards harmony, complexity and creativity. Here, God is luring us toward healing – a perspective that may offer fresh insights into each of the 12 Steps.

Open-and-Relational Theology and the 12 Steps

Open-and-Relational Theology emphasizes that God experiences life with us in real time, responding with love and inviting relationship rather than imposing control. This section explores how this view of God as responsive and deeply involved can transform how we walk each of the 12 Steps. Open-and-Relational theology is similar to Process Theology but poses an even more intimate connection to the Divine.

Chapter 20
Traditional and Progressive Christianity Compared on the 12 Steps

Introduction: Two Lenses on the Path of Healing

The 12 Steps of Alcoholics Anonymous speak a spiritual language broad enough to include people from every background. Yet, when people approach these steps through a Christian lens, they often encounter very different visions of who God is, how change happens, and what recovery really means.

Traditional Christianity, shaped by doctrines emphasizing sin, judgment, and divine sovereignty, tends to view the 12 Steps through the lens of moral failure, repentance, and divine rescue. In this view, God is often portrayed as the all-powerful ruler who intervenes to save and sanctify those who submit.

Progressive Christianity, shaped by values of inclusion, relational theology, and divine love, sees the 12 Steps as invitations into honesty, vulnerability, relationship, and co-creation. Here, God is envisioned as deeply relational, walking beside us and inspiring us to find healing and wholeness.

What follows is a short exploration of each of the 12 Steps through both lenses. This is not to diminish one view or exalt the other. Rather, it offers a compassionate and honest reflection on how these theological differences shape the recovery journey.

Step One — Admitting Powerlessness
"We admitted we were powerless over alcohol — that our lives had become unmanageable."

Traditional View:

Powerlessness is often tied to sin and total depravity. Human beings, in this view, are inherently broken and sinful, needing to be saved by a sovereign God. Admitting powerlessness is seen as confessing sinfulness and acknowledging one's helpless state apart from divine intervention.

Progressive View:

Powerlessness is seen not as moral failure but as sacred honesty. In this view, addiction is a complex interplay of trauma, biology, and social factors — not merely sin. Admitting powerlessness is the courageous beginning of surrendering illusions of control and opening to relational healing with God, self, and others.

Step Two — Coming to Believe
"Came to believe that a Power greater than ourselves could restore us to sanity."

Traditional View:

Belief is most often understood as doctrinal assent — accepting the truth about God, Jesus, salvation and scriptural authority. In essence, right belief leads to right recovery. Restoration is framed as being saved from sin and brought into the correct standing before God.

Progressive View:

Belief is relational trust, not rigid doctrine. Scripture is inspirational and insightful. To "come to believe" is to become open to divine possibility and compassionate presence. Restoration is about returning to wholeness and sanity through divine companionship, not just moral correction.

Step Three — Turning Our Will Over
"Made a decision to turn our will and our lives over to the care of God as we understood Him."

Traditional View:

Turning over one's will is often understood as total submission to God's authority. It emphasizes surrendering to God's sovereign plan and abandoning self-reliance in favor of divine control as the ultimate path to recovery.

Progressive View:

Turning over one's will is about aligning with God's loving presence rather than submitting to domination. It is choosing relationship over isolation, and trusting that divine care invites — not forces — us toward life and healing.

Step Four — Moral Inventory
"Made a searching and fearless moral inventory of ourselves."

Traditional View:

This searching and fearless personal inventory of our past focuses on sin and all manner of dishonesty and ethical failures. The emphasis is on confessing wrongdoing to avoid divine punishment and restore moral purity.

Progressive View:

The inventory is about truth-telling and self-awareness, not self-condemnation or punishment. It involves naming harm, acknowledging wounds, and trusting that God receives our honesty with love, not judgment.

Step Five — Admitting Wrongs
"Admitted to God, to ourselves, and to another human being the exact nature of our wrongs."

Traditional View:

Confession is often viewed as a necessary step to avoid eternal separation from God. It restores the sinner to a state of grace and right relationship after serious moral failure.

Progressive View:

Confession is about relational healing. Admitting wrongs is not about avoiding punishment but about repairing trust and reestablishing honesty with self, God, and community.

Step Six — Ready for Change
"Were entirely ready to have God remove all these defects of character."

Traditional View:

Being humble and ready is seen as the precursor to repentance — a decisive turning from sin and ego and in turn renouncing destructive desires. The key is trusting that God will sanctify and cleanse the penitent heart.

Progressive View:

Readiness is relational and gradual. God does not remove defects magically but invites us to partner in letting go of what no longer serves our healing. Readiness is about open willingness, not spiritual perfection.

Step Seven — Humbly Asking
"Humbly asked Him to remove our shortcomings."

Traditional View:

This is often seen as an act of humble submission to divine will, asking for deliverance from sinful patterns through divine intervention. Our moral inventory is in essence corrected by an omnipotent holy father.

Progressive View:

Asking humbly is about inviting God to co-restore and co-create with us. Shortcomings are not marks of shame but areas where healing is needed. God works with us gently, not by force, to reshape our wayward character.

Step Eight — Making the List
"Made a list of all persons we had harmed and became willing to make amends to them all."

Traditional View:

The emphasis here is often on righting wrongs and recognizing our broken earthly relationships. The goal is avoiding divine disfavor and demonstrating first steps to repentance.

Progressive View:

Making the list is about relational justice and moral reflection. It's not about appeasing God, but about courageously naming harm so that repair and restoration can be pursued in earnest.

Step Nine — Making Amends
"Made direct amends wherever possible, except when to do so would injure them or others."

Traditional View:

Amends may be seen as restitution for sin, fulfilling a moral and or divine obligation to correct wrongs and restore righteousness. Amends are made in the eyes of a judgmental God.

Progressive View:

Amends are restorative acts of love and repair. They are not about earning forgiveness but about participating in God's healing work in the world, guided by humility and compassion.

Step Ten — Daily Inventory
"Continued to take personal inventory and when we were wrong promptly admitted it."

Traditional View:

Daily inventory reinforces vigilance against sin and promotes ongoing repentance to remain in right standing with God. The rules of divine justice inspire righteous, consistent behavior.

Progressive View:

Daily inventory is about staying spiritually honest and relationally open. It is grounded in self-compassion, not fear, and helps us stay aligned with God's ideal of growth and harmony.

Step Eleven — Conscious Contact

"Sought through prayer and meditation to improve our conscious contact with God..."

Traditional View:

Prayer is often understood as submission to God's will, seeking divine commands and pledging obedience. Petitioning prayer can ask for specific guidance in a person's life, or request intervention – the hand of God – in a situation.

Progressive View:

Prayer and meditation are about relationship, not performance or request. Conscious contact is an ongoing dialogue of love, mutuality, and trust with a God who listens, responds, and invites us into deeper awareness and inspired behavior.

Step Twelve — Carrying the Message

"Having had a spiritual awakening as the result of these steps, we tried to carry this message to alcoholics..."

Traditional View:

Carrying the message can be seen as evangelistic duty — saving others from sin and pointing them to doctrinal truth. This can also be seen as a form of Christian witness — faith lived out in community of the suffering.

Progressive View:

Carrying the message is about sharing hope, healing, and love. It is less about converting others and more about witnessing to the grace that has transformed us, and inviting others to join in the ongoing work of restoration.

Conclusion: Traditional and Progressive; Different Lenses, Shared Grace

Traditional and Progressive Christian approaches to the 12 Steps offer very different theological visions. One emphasizes obedience to divine authority, moral vigilance, and deliverance from sin. And it asks us to read scripture as both real and true. It also emphasizes that Christian witness is an active, engaging practice. The Progressive Christianity emphasizes relational honesty, divine companionship, and participation in ongoing healing and love. Per scripture, we are asked to find what is universally true, rather than what is factual or literally "real." And here, Christian witness is about attraction and example rather than promotion or coercion.

For those shaped by Progressive Christianity, the Steps become not just tools for overcoming addiction, but invitations to trust that God meets us where we are, walks with us daily, and subtly encourages us — step by step — into deeper love, freedom, and connection.

While these lenses contrast in many ways, they are united by one profound truth: recovery is a spiritual journey. Both paths point toward transformation, humility, and grace.

Chapter 21
Process Theology
Applied to the 12 Steps

Introduction: Dynamic Love and Divine Partnership in Recovery

The spiritual path of recovery is not a one-size-fits-all journey. While many people find comfort in the general language of a 'Higher Power,' others long for deeper theological reflection to help them connect more meaningfully with the divine presence that guides them through the 12 Steps. For those who bring a Christian background — especially from progressive traditions — two approaches to theology can offer valuable insight: Process Theology and Open and Relational Theology.

Both of these theologies emphasize relationship, divine love, human freedom, and the unfolding nature of spiritual growth. Unlike more traditional doctrines that may depict God as distant, impassive, or controlling, Process and Open and Relational thinkers describe God as deeply involved with creation, responsive to our experiences, and always inviting us forward without force, coercion or judgment.

These brief reflections offer perspectives on how two fresh views of God and reality align with the wisdom of the 12 Steps. They are intended for those who desire to explore new theological meaning alongside their recovery work. For some, these insights may be helpful companions from the start; for others, they may be most useful after walking through the steps practically and personally, first. Engage them as an invitation to learn more, knowing they are here to offer an alternative perspective—not to complicate or burden your journey.

This chapter will focus on the forms of Christianity which are best described as espousing Process Theologies; the next chapter will focus on forms of Christianity which are best described as espousing Open and Relational Theologies.

Process Theology and the 12 Steps

Process Theology offers a view of God that is dynamic, relational, and ever-evolving. Instead of seeing God as an all-controlling force, Process thinkers describe God as the cosmic lure toward beauty, truth, and goodness. God is not coercive but persuasive, calling creation — including us — into greater wholeness, harmony and complexity. In recovery, this means God is not fixing us by force. God is subtly inviting us into change.

Process Theology and Addiction Recovery

Process Theology is grounded in the philosophical vision of Alfred North Whitehead and others who affirm that:

- *Reality is dynamic and relational, not static or fixed.*
- *God is in process with us, constantly affected by and responding to the world.*
- *God does not control outcomes but offers each moment the best possible next step, called the "initial aim."*
- *The world is a web of interconnected becoming, and God is the source of creativity and transformation within it.*

When applied to recovery, Process Theology portrays God not as a remote judge or a one-time savior, but as the ever-present source of healing possibilities, always luring us toward wholeness and freedom in the midst of our struggle.

Step-by-Step: The 12 Steps through a Process Theology Lens

Step 1: We admitted we were powerless over alcohol — that our lives had become unmanageable.
God's Role (Process View):

God does not cause suffering or addiction but feels its full impact with us. In every moment, God offers a new possibility, even in our lowest places. This step is the beginning of aligning with God's lure toward truth, honesty, and healing — even in collapse.

Step 2: Came to believe that a Power greater than ourselves could restore us to sanity.
God's Role (Process View):

In Process Theology, God is not a dominating force outside reality but the very essence of it — always offering healing possibilities. Belief in this Power means trusting that every moment carries divine potential for sanity, balance, and a better way forward.

Step 3: Made a decision to turn our will and our lives over to the care of God as we understood Him.
God's Role (Process View):

God does not control our will, but entices us toward harmony and healing. This "turning over" is not surrender to domination but cooperation with divine creativity. God's "care" is the gentle, persuasive invitation toward greater well-being in every evolving moment.

Step 4: Made a searching and fearless moral inventory of ourselves.
God's Role (Process View):

God is not compiling a list of our failures but is along side us as we examine our past with courage. God is the lure toward self-awareness and integrity, helping us integrate our past without shame and moving us toward a more honest self-in-process.

Step 5: Admitted to God, to ourselves, and to another human being the exact nature of our wrongs.
God's Role (Process View):

Process Theology sees confession as relational alignment. God is not waiting to punish, but receiving our truth with compassionate understanding. This step deepens the process of becoming — God responds to our honesty by weaving it into the ongoing work of healing.

Step 6: Were entirely ready to have God remove all these defects of character.
God's Role (Process View):

God cannot forcibly remove anything from us. Instead, God offers us a vision of who we could become and gently encourages us to move in that direction. Readiness means becoming attuned to that call — to the next best version of ourselves, which God is always proposing.

Step 7: Humbly asked Him to remove our shortcomings.
God's Role (Process View):

God never imposes change but is always inviting us toward transformation through love and freedom. Asking God to "remove" our shortcomings is about synchronizing our will with divine possibility —

partnering with God to grow toward our unfolding potential.

Step 8: Made a list of all persons we had harmed, and became willing to make amends to them all.
God's Role (Process View):

God supports the moral imagination needed for this step. In Process Theology, relationships are central — what we do ripples through others, including the "consequent nature" of God. In-turn we are called to be co-healers, drawing us toward relational harmony and balance.

Step 9: Made direct amends to such people wherever possible, except when to do so would injure them or others.
God's Role (Process View):

God is present in each courageous step toward justice and repair. Amends reflect God's ongoing goal of co-healing with creation. God rejoices not just in the act, but in the becoming — in our movement from brokenness toward reconciliation and relational integrity.

Step 10: Continued to take personal inventory and when we were wrong promptly admitted it.
God's Role (Process View):

Process Theology affirms that we are never finished. Each moment brings a new divine invitation. God is the guide who walks beside us, calling us to honesty not out of guilt but as part of our continual evolution toward love, truth, and justice.

Step 11: Sought through prayer and meditation to improve our conscious contact with God...
God's Role (Process View):

In Process Theology, prayer is co-creative communication. God is not silent or absent, but intimately involved in our evolution. Conscious contact is about tuning into divine possibilities, the "initial aim," and growing in sensitivity to God's ideal of goodness.

Step 12: Having had a spiritual awakening… we tried to carry this message… and to practice these principles in all our affairs.
God's Role (Process View):

Awakening is the fruit of a shared process—our openness and God's persistent call toward beauty and justice. Now, God invites us to become agents of healing for others. Our recovery is not just personal but participatory in the divine creative advance of the world.

Recovery as the Art of Becoming

Process Theology reminds us that God is not behind us, pushing, nor above us, judging—but with us, moment by moment, offering new possibilities. In recovery:

- *God is the Source of Freshness in every decision.*
- *God does not apply supernatural power but works with human (and all) nature.*
- *God is not a rescuer from outside reality, but a co-creator of new futures.*
- *God is wounded with us, rejoices in our growth, and never gives up offering a better next step.*

Each step is not a ladder to perfection but an unfolding journey, where God's love is not static or transactional but dynamic, healing, and full of creative potential. In every moment, God whispers: "There is a better way. Let's take this step together."

Chapter 22
Open and Relational Theology (ORT) and the 12 Steps

As you read the this chapter, you'll find that Open-and-Relational theology has many similarities to Process Theology, and yet there are subtle but important differences. Open-and-Relational Theology emphasizes God's responsiveness and relationality. God experiences the world in real time, feeling our joys and suffering alongside us. Importantly, God does not and cannot preordain outcomes or override human freedom. In recovery, this view reassures us that God is dynamically involved, loving us in our messiness and always offering new paths forward –without literally manipulating or reducing our human agency.

Open and Relational Theology and Addiction Recovery

Open and Relational Theology, a faith understanding popularized by author, professor and theologian Thomas Oord, affirms that:

- *God is love, relational, and not coercive.*
- *The future is open – not predetermined even by God.*
- *God works in partnership with creation, including people in recovery.*
- *Human choices matter and God responds creatively and faithfully to them.*

When applied to recovery, ORT portrays God not as a distant judge, micromanager or determinant of the future, but as a companion who suffers with us, empowers our agency, and responds in real time to our pain, surrender, and growth.

Step-by-Step: The 12 Steps through an Open and Relational Lens

Step 1: We admitted we were powerless over alcohol — that our lives had become unmanageable.
God's Role (ORT View):

God lovingly invites honesty without shame. Rather than orchestrating suffering to "teach a lesson," God is present in our powerlessness, aching with us and actively oriented toward wholeness. God does not force change but celebrates this moment of clarity and openness.

Step 2: Came to believe that a Power greater than ourselves could restore us to sanity.
God's Role (ORT View):

God is not a manipulative force, but an ever-present source of hope. ORT emphasizes that God cannot heal us without our participation, but is always offering possibilities of transformation. This is not about magical intervention but divine collaboration.

Step 3: Made a decision to turn our will and our lives over to the care of God as we understood Him.
God's Role (ORT View):

In ORT, God does not override our will but welcomes our consent to deeper partnership. This step becomes a mutual relationship, where surrender doesn't mean erasure but a joining of purpose. God's care is active, responsive, and always respectful of our freedom.

Step 4: Made a searching and fearless moral inventory of ourselves.
God's Role (ORT View):

God is not keeping a ledger of our sins but supportively walks beside us as we face our inner reality. God's role is that of an empathetic truth-teller and healer, encouraging courageous self-reflection without fear of rejection. God helps us see ourselves truly and compassionately.

Step 5: Admitted to God, to ourselves, and to another human being the exact nature of our wrongs.
God's Role (ORT View):

ORT emphasizes that God already knows and still loves us — but our sharing matters because truth-telling restores relationships. God is present in the sacred act of confession, not as a judge demanding penance, but as a wounded healer rejoicing in intimacy and honesty.

Step 6: Were entirely ready to have God remove all these defects of character.
God's Role (ORT View):

God cannot unilaterally "remove" character defects — not because of unwillingness, but because of love that honors human agency. God is always working with us, helping us to let go of what binds us and co-creating new habits, choices, and ways of being.

Step 7: Humbly asked Him to remove our shortcomings.
God's Role (ORT View):

God receives our humility as a mutual act of trust, not subjugation. In ORT, God's power is persuasive, not coercive, so this is a request for deep inner cooperation — God works with the grain of our will to grow and inspire real transformation.

Step 8: Made a list of all persons we had harmed, and became willing to make amends to them all.
God's Role (ORT View):

God empowers empathy and moral imagination. ORT sees God as drawing us into redemptive relationships. God's grace shows us the importance of interconnected healing, not only personal forgiveness. God supports us in this sometimes painful readiness to repair.

Step 9: Made direct amends to such people wherever possible, except when to do so would injure them or others.
God's Role (ORT View):

God is present in the courage to restore, not out of obligation but of liberating love. ORT views God as a non-coercive reconciler, always working toward restored relationships. God is both comforter, companion and empathetic guide in the hard work of reconciliation.

Step 10: Continued to take personal inventory and when we were wrong promptly admitted it.
God's Role (ORT View):

God is not looking for perfection, but for faithful responsiveness. ORT holds that God is always inviting and encouraging us into real-time growth and correction. God does not "keep score," but partners with us in ongoing relational integrity.

Step 11: Sought through prayer and meditation to improve our conscious contact with God…
God's Role (ORT View):

God is always seeking connection, but never forces it. ORT emphasizes mutual relationship — prayer becomes a living dialogue, not a transaction. God's guidance is not fixed or controlling, but dynamic and attuned to the moment. Conscious contact deepens trust and discernment.

Step 12: Having had a spiritual awakening… we tried to carry this message… and to practice these principles in all our affairs.
God's Role (ORT View):

The awakening is co-authored — God plants the seeds, but we help them grow. God rejoices in our healing and calls us to become co-healers in the world. ORT views Step 12 as the fruit of divine partnership, where we become vessels of grace in service to others.

ORT Framing Conclusion: Recovery as Divine Co-Creation

Open and Relational Theology reveals recovery not as something God does to us, but as something God does with us. God is neither absent nor overpowering — God is lovingly persuasive, infinitely patient, and always responsive. In recovery, God is:

- *Not the puppet master but the companion.*
- *Not the punisher but the restorer.*
- *Not the fixer but the faithful co-creator of new life.*
- *Not the designer of the future, but the possibility of a better future.*

Each step becomes a dialogue with the Divine, an ongoing process of healing that honors our freedom, fosters responsibility, and is suffused with hope that never gives up.

Conclusion
A Spacious and Loving God for the Journey

Whether viewed through the lens of Process Theology or an Open and Relational Theology, the God revealed in recovery is relational, persuasive, and compassionate. This God does not dominate but invites. This God does not fix from afar but co-creates healing with us, moment by moment.

Progressive Christian approaches remind us that God is not found in shame, fear, or rigid formulas — but in honesty, mutuality, and love. Recovery, through the 12 Steps, becomes not only a pathway out of addiction, but a sacred pilgrimage into divine relationship and understanding.

The divine lure is always present, whispering: "Come as you are. Let's walk this together."

Moving Forward with Your Own Understanding of Grace

Theological reflection does not offer all the answers, but it does offer us language for the journey. Whether you find resonance in Traditional, Progressive, Process, or Open-and-Relational understandings of God, each perspective provides insight into how divine love and human transformation meet.

The 12 Steps ask us to become honest, to trust, to repair, and to grow. The God who meets us in these steps is not far off. This God walks with us, invites us, and co-creates healing in our lives moment by moment. May these reflections not burden you with ideas, but free you to know that grace takes many forms — and that at every step, divine encouragement always surrounds you, sometimes whispering, sometimes resonating in the voices around us: "Keep going. I am with you."

The God Who Walks With And Within Us

Recovery is not just about abstaining from a substance or a behavior. It's about becoming whole — spiritually, emotionally, and relationally. And at the heart of that transformation lies a profound invitation: to discover, or rediscover, a Higher Power that can walk with us through the 12 Steps.

For some, that Higher Power has always been God — a source of comfort, strength, and hope. For others, the very word "God" feels loaded with pain, rejection, or confusion. This book has not tried to resolve that tension with easy answers or obvious alternatives. Instead, it has tried to hold space for a journey — a sacred, often messy, spiritual unfolding.

What the 12 Steps offer is not a theology, but a path. What progressive Christianity offers is not dogma, but a vision of God big enough to hold our doubts, our wounds, and our desire for healing. Through the lens of Jesus — the one who touched lepers, welcomed outcasts, and embodied grace — we are invited into a relationship with the Divine that is compassionate, liberating, and deeply personal.

The views explored in this book — progressive Christianity, Process Theology, and Open-and-Relational Theology — are not rejections of traditional faith. They are not critiques for the sake of critique. They are invitations. Invitations for those who have been harmed by narrow theologies. Invitations for those whose image of God has become a barrier instead of a bridge. Invitations to see the Higher Power in the Steps not as a distant judge, but as a present, evolving, loving companion.

Traditional Christian understandings have brought healing and strength to many. But for others, they have been a source of shame, exclusion, or spiritual paralysis. If that's your story, know this: You are not faithless. You are not broken. You are simply being called to seek God in a new way — a way that is honest, relational, and rooted in grace.

In the theological understandings we have touched on in this book, God is not an unmovable, controlling force but a living, loving presence who lures us toward healing, who suffers with us, and who invites us to co-create our future. In these expansive Christian faith orientations, God does not dictate every detail of our lives but responds with us, dynamically and lovingly, in real time. These perspectives do not dismiss the God of tradition — they simply widen the lens, allowing us to see more clearly the God who has always been there, even when we couldn't name or trust that presence.

The 12 Steps ask us to believe in a power greater than ourselves. They ask us to surrender control, to make amends, to seek ongoing spiritual growth. None of that is possible without some vision of grace — a grace that doesn't wait for perfection, but meets us where we are.

So, what matters is not what you call your Higher Power. What matters is whether that power brings you into deeper truth, connection, and transformation. Whether it calls you toward the person you were meant to be — sober, honest, free, and loved.

If the God of your past made you feel small, unwanted, or afraid, let this be the moment you step toward something new. Let Jesus be your guide, not your judge. Let grace be your rhythm, not your reward. Let your Higher Power — whatever name you use — be a wellspring of mercy, strength, and sacred presence.

And remember: You don't have to have it all figured out. You just have to be willing. Step by step, grace will meet you. And so will God — in every surrender, in every inventory, in every moment of truth, hope, and healing.

You are not alone. Not now. Not ever. Amen.